AF424366

HYPNOTIC BEATBOXING

Hypnotic Beatboxing Techniques That Can Improve Your Mental Health and Life

MICHAEL BOLTON JR.

To Grace and Lucas,

I love you and am proud of you!

Advisement

I am not a doctor and these techniques do not cure or treat any disease. If you are having any physical or mental health problems, you should first seek licensed professional help. The techniques in this book can help with mental health challenges such as anxiety and depression, but are not to be taken in place of medicine or other therapies. Do not stop taking prescription medicine prescribed by a doctor without first consulting with a doctor first. If you are in a crisis call an emergency hotline or 911.

-Michael Bolton Jr.

- In 2011 I was looking for an alternate way to cope with mental health issues. In a used bookstore I found a book that would change my thinking forever. It introduced me to the world of Hypnosis.
- In this chapter we will look at Hypnotic Beatboxing's definition and roots.

Origins of Hypnotic Beatboxing

The concept for Hypnotic Beatboxing runs back to 2011 at a used bookstore in Owatonna, Minnesota. I was in a manic phase of my life and I stumbled upon a book called "Helping Yourself with Autogenics". It was a pioneer book on the practice of self-hypnosis. The suggestions and explanations in that book were life-changing for me. I was intrigued by the quit smoking process. I found the relaxation aspect of hypnosis and self-hypnosis to be extremely helpful. I was grateful that I happened upon that book when I was acquiring a taste for knowledge.

The most powerful method of Hypnotic Beatboxing is adding formulas to a beat. This method is based off of a beatboxing technique pioneered by beatboxer named "Kid Lucky". The technique is called beat rhyming. Beat rhyming is when you are beatboxing and singing at the same time. It is done by spacing a pattern of beatbox sounds with words or phrases in between them. In later parts of this book this method will be shown with actual hypnotic or hypnoboxics formulas.

Fast forward to the year 2018, I was recording my first self-hypnotic beatbox. I made a video in the previous winter of 2017 about Hypnotic Beatboxing and brought to light the implications of using beatboxing to help with relaxation and hypnosis. I recorded my first Hypnotic Beatboxing MP3 January 8th 2018 I made it available on the web.

Not much had happened from that MP3 but it sparked an interest in me to keep pursuing this hypnotic application of beatboxing. In 2019 I was reinventing the scene of beatboxing into writing form. Now in 2020 I am putting this practice into play in people's lives.

Hypnoboxics is based off of the Greek word *Hypnos* or sleep and *Boxics* stands for the beatboxing aspect of making the sounds. Together they make the therapy or technique of Hypnoboxics. Hypnoboxics can be used to help cope with anxiety, stress, depression, anger and other emotional challenges as a coping skill. This should be used in conjunction with other coping skills such as therapies, and medications if, and when necessary. But Hypnoboxics is a bit of a mouthful, and may be a little harder to recall in a conversation. Even though it is built off of an intriguing science or pseudoscience it is just not as catchy as, "Hypnotic Beatboxing"

Hypnosis is an origin for Hypnotic Beatboxing. In hypnosis and Hypnotic Beatboxing, the power of the subconscious mind is utilized. It is from the deep relaxation you receive the potent verbal formulas of change. This is how you can really make a difference in your life. Hypnotic Beatboxing is for coping with stress but can also work as a tool for depression, anxiety and addictions.

Later on I will describe how to put formulas in between basic beatbox sounds. Hypnotic Beatboxing is a branch of a tree called **Applied Beatboxing**. Applied Beatboxing is beatboxing for practical and application based purposes. Within the branch of Applied Beatboxing there is a branch called **Psychoboxics**. Psychoboxics is based off the Greek word *psycho* which refers to mind or brain, and the word *boxics* which represents beatboxing in general. There is yet another field with in applied beatboxing. It is called

Pneumoboxics. Pneumoboxics is based off of the Greek word *pneumos* lung or air, and the word *boxics* represents beatboxing aspects. Pneumoboxics is a broad therapy or technique of coping skills based off of breathing made with beatboxing sounds. For this particular book we will focus solely on Hypnotic Beatboxing and the benefits thereof.

Mind-Body Connection

There are long associations with good health in the body equating that a healthy mind translates into a healthy body. One must not underestimate how much the mind can make a person be healthy or sick when given the right or wrong kind of thoughts. The mind can be given suggestions by us to ourselves or by others. These suggestions are hypnotic or suggestive. They can happen while we are unaware or completely aware. For hypnosis or Hypnotic Beatboxing to be successful it taps into the subconscious mind. The unconscious mind is able to work and enhance and make changes without having to fight our deepest behavioral and negative thought processes.

Bio Feedback

Biofeedback is the thing that goes into our mind in the background while we are unaware. This could be a buzzing fan playing in your house. That fan is blowing air on you from a distance and your mind absorbs that sound. At the same time, you hear your kids screaming. While the screaming is going on, the fan fades out. You no longer notice the fan. It has become subconscious. Hypnosis or Hypnotic Beatboxing suggestions work the same way. They are a blanket in the background that bathes your mind. You are able to receive suggestions while you are relaxed and may not be actually paying attention deliberately. Your unconscious mind is absorbing the thoughts like a video camera or an audio recorder.

A New Form of Breathing Exercise

Hypnotic Beatboxing has largely to do with breathing. It is one of the main modes of effect for this form of hypnosis. In so many therapies and techniques breathing is a crucial aspect of coping. It is the breathing that causes the relaxation necessary for hypnosis or Hypnotic Beatboxing to be effective in making change in one's life.

Total Relaxation

Hypnosis **Definition**: *As implied by the word Hypnos which means sleep in Greek, hypnoboxics is about complete relaxation. Using this technique can create a deep relaxation and is designed to cause a peaceful mind.* This is a facet also that is similar to traditional hypnosis. It is in the deep relaxation that changes change are brought forth in your life.

Programming

So much of our lives have subtle and overt programming. This programming goes deeper than just hearing or seeing things. Your brain has massive networks of neurons. These are designed to help the way your brain processes things. There are like a hard drive that stores memories, feelings, and the way you think. In life we have people tell us what to do from an early age. Your parents may say things to scare you into behaving. Some people face abusive language. Others have more helpful and encouraging families and friends. But if you hear enough negative feedback about yourself in the world around you from your family and loved ones it can have a lasting effect. These suggestions can create a memory associated feeling that affects you throughout your life.

The news tells you that it is the end of the world and that bad things are happening everywhere. The loom and doom of media has commentators and health "experts" feed tell us about our inadequacies or bad habits. Social media pushes materialism and excess and gratuitous lifestyle. To many people this may seem fun but it actually is suggesting in our life that we need these things or are missing out.

Be aware of the subtle programming of that commercial for the best razor or the food that you love. They are placing a want or need in your mind. Is it very important to have a peaceful, calm, and a wise mind when addressing the needs of your life.

It is crucial e mindful of the things you allow yourself to take in for mental digestion. The programming in this book is designed to be helpful to you. It is designed with your benefit in mind. You will find ways to write your own programs of the mind through powerful positive formulas.

Power of Suggestion

In everyday life there are so many areas of suggestions. These suggestions take form of media, entertainment, advertisement and even things we say to ourselves. A commercial tells says you need "this" product because it is "better" than the others. Your friend suggests something they like and that you should "try" it. The news tells you things are going badly and that we need to get more of something or do less of something.

Everyday we hear about things that we need or things that we do not have. People tell you how to think. We tell our kids how to do something. Everywhere there are suggestions. Not every time you hear a suggestion do you except or fall into it. Despite this fact, it is planted in your head. It is important to note these things but also know the role of your subconscious mind. The subconscious mind is your unaware thoughts in the back of your mind. It is here that most strongly affects your choices. In the subconscious mind, deep programming and reprogramming really begins to solidify in your life. This is true with habits and is true with desire and fear. Hypnotic Beatboxing or traditional hypnosis works on this subconscious area of the mind. So be mindful of the power that suggestion has in your mind and life.

Power of an Affirmation

The things that we say to ourselves go a long way in how we behave, act, and think. The things we say to ourselves can be verbal or not vocalized. The first one is obvious. When you say something to yourself out loud it is verbal. More subtly is when you say something to yourself in your head by way of thought it is non-verbal. These types of things are very much an affirmation. The definition of an affirmation is as follows: *the action or process of affirming something or being affirmed.*

When you affirm something, you aknowledge and reinforce it. Affirmations can be both negative and positive. Positive affirmations are empowering and help improve life. A negative affirmation can tend to reinforce negative thoughts and behavioral patterns. A positive affirmation tends to create feelings of adequacy and successfulness. A negative affirmation tends to create empty and negative feelings. These feelings affect our outcomes in life. You may say something to yourself like, "I will never be good enough" or "I will always be overweight." These types of statements tend to make it difficult to accept yourself or in the latter try to lose weight.

Try to say, "I am good enough. I am complete." Or

"I can and will lose weight."

Our brains are designed to record these things. Recording good statements as a positive affirmation in your mind is a very important way to approach things. In hypnosis traditionally and Hypnotic Beatboxing, the formulas and patterns use, are solely positive affirmations. It is important to leave out any negative affirmations and replace them with positive ones.

WHY HYPNOTIC BEATBOXING?

- Traditional Hypnosis has a long standing and growing body of evidence to bolster its effectiveness for living a healthier life. I have pioneered Hypnotic Beatboxing over the last three years making multiple revisions to the technique. Hypnotic Beatboxing has much of the same promises based on the fact that the methods are similar.
- In this chapter we will explore how Hypnotic beatboxing can be beneficial and why.

While the benefits of Hypnotic Beatboxing are similar to traditional hypnosis, there may be some added benefits. Beatboxing works heavily on the breathing and can benefit the circulatory and respiratory systems of a person. For the most simplified explanation and list of benefits we stick to mental health resolutions. Hypnotic Beatboxing can be a great tool for coping with mental illness issues such as stress, depression, and anxiety. I have found that when I have been very angry, anxious, stressed or depressed Hypnotic Beatboxing is helpful. It is very effective to do a simple rhythm and words of affirmation to calm down. This is a first-hand example of how doing a rhythm and beat can be effective to calm someone down when are having mental anguish.

On the note of physical benefits when you are less stressed your body tends to feel better and be healthier. It is for this reason that doing a regular regimen of Hypnotic

Beatboxing may very well help you have better physical health. There are studies about beatboxing helping the physical body but much research needs to be done to verify effectiveness. For the sake of this book we will focus on the mental health and behavioural wellness from the application of Hypnotic Beatboxing.

A Trip to The Dentist

It was November 2nd 2020 and I found myself in the dentist's office filled with dread. My anxiety was through the roof as I was getting my teeth cleaned. Before I went in I knew my anxiety was going to be strong. I debated whether I would take an anti-anxiety med as needed beforehand. I opted not to take it and was in the seat starting to get extremely anxious. It was too late to take my med and I did not want to be tired. A lot of times the anti-anxiety meds create a sedation. It is from that sedation that causes the peacefulness the meds can give. That peacefulness is a night and day difference from the anxiety someone might suffer from disorders or situations. Going to the dentist is quite often an undesirable place to be for many people. I had taken my daughter there a month or so before and she was three years old and she was just terrified.

As the dental hygienist began to probe in my mouth. I got shaky and scared. It was so awful. Yet I still did not want to take my as needed anti-anxiety med. So the options were to suffer the anxiety and fight the whole time to not think about it, or to root it out by way of reasoning. These were not really likely to be successful options, at least not for the dealing my intense anxiety. I noticed that I was thinking of my technique called The Heartbeat Breath and I did a little grunt. That grunt became a couple short little hums. The hums became a heartbeat or a throat kick. This technique will be discussed later on in the book. This breathing technique caused me such a piece that inspired me to add this to the book. It completely eradicated my anxiety. I felt a little awkward so I explained to the hygienist what I was doing. She thought I was just falling asleep, so it was a little laughable. With an effective coping skill most of us can get through just about any issue we have.

Deep Relaxation

In hypnosis or Hypnotic Beatboxing you will find a lot about deep relaxation. Often the words "deep" or "deeper" are used in formulas. The formulas used are designed to cause you to go into a very tranquil mind often empty of thoughts and open to suggestion. It is important to note that in hypnosis or Hypnotic Beatboxing you are always in control and can awake or be alert and focused and tend to things if need arises. The relaxation that Hypnotic Beatboxing and hypnosis provides is astounding and very well enjoyed by many.

Anyone who has a mouth, tongue, teeth, nose, lungs, and lips can do Hypnotic Beatboxing. Barring some debilitating impediment either physical or mental most anybody can do Hypnotic Beatboxing. If you have anxiety or depression, addictions, stress or just want to have a positive relaxation, Hypnotic Beatboxing can benefit you.

There are people who would say "I can not be hypnotized." For the skeptics I offer this. If you can tell yourself something, believe it, and do it-then you can do hypnosis. All hypnosis is self-hypnosis. You are choosing to relax when you do Hypnotic Beatboxing. All Hypnotic Beatboxng is self-Hypnotic Beatboxing. If you say you "can", you "can". If you say you "can't", you "can't". You choose what to believe when you tell yourself something. If you choose to relax, that is a choice you willingly make. If you choose to make a change in your life, that is a choice you willingly make. When you engage in Hypnotic Beatboxing or hypnosis you are choosing to be willing to relax and or make changes in your life.

One has to be motivated in their life in any particular area to excel in that particular area. Hypnoboxics is a skill, there are very simplified parts of or applications for it. The more skilled you are at doing beats, or drum sounds, or sound effects in general the more skilled you will be at Hypnotic Beatboxing. You can do more when you know more sounds. But even one sound only you can do an intermediate skill level with just a few moments of time. Hypnotic beatboxing, just like any other skill, builds on itself with practice. The common saying is "progress not perfection." You want to progress in your life. Perfectionism has a tendency to be very unhealthy. No one is perfect, and perfection is a standard we cannot reach. But we can reach progress. We can reach great mountain peaks of progress. To grow in life, one must progress in a positive fashion. Seek progress.

Hypnotic Beatboxing vs. Hypnosis

Traditional hypnosis uses verbal formulas and often ambient background music to cause a relaxation. Formulas are often geared towards personal change and betterment.

Hypnotic Beatboxing uses verbalized formulas as well as well as beats or beatbox sounds. It can often be done by the person using it. It can be self-administered. One can also have a hypnotherapist do it for them. It is a relatively new technique in the realms of hypnosis. Hypnotic beatboxing can be geared at personal change and betterment as well as it can be very relaxing.

Words Only-Hypnosis.

Traditional hypnosis is based largely on only on usage of words. Traditional hypnosis can use ambient background music but the words are where the power is.

Words and Beats by Voice Only-Hypnotic Beatboxing

In Hypnotic Beatboxing one uses beatboxing sounds which are from the voice and mouth as well as a of use verbal formulas. Both hypnosis and Hypnotic beatboxing use words only. Hypnotic Beatboxing relies on voice only to make the background music or soundscapes as well. While it can be done by voice only, it can also be recorded.

Patterns

In Hypnotic Beatboxing (Hypnoboxics" often it is best to do a short rhythm of drum sounds with a couple words of affirmation. This is simple enough to accomplish, yet potent enough to create positive change in a person's life.

Formulas

Formulas in Hypnotic Beatboxing very similarly resemble traditional hypnosis. They use strong authoritative and calming language. They empower the listener or in the case of Hypnotic Beatboxing the person is doing the beat formula to have positive changes in their life. These formulas are comprised of beats and or sounds and words. The application and how to compose formulas will be discussed later.

Batteries Not Necessary

Unlike regular Hypnosis, which now is able to be played off of Mp3 or with a Hypnotherapist on a video. Hypnotic Beatboxing does not need batteries or electricity to be done. It does not even require another person to deliver it. So this autonomous form of hypnosis is energy free. So it can be done anywhere with or without a device.

The Role of Traditional Beatboxing

Hypnotic Beatboxing is a therapeutic technique of breathing. It uses common beatboxing sounds to create therapeutic effects. Traditional beatboxing is drums and instruments sounds geared almost entirely at entertainment. Both traditional beatboxing and Hypnotic Beatboxing use beatboxing (percussive and instrument) sounds, but Hypnotic Beatboxing focuses on a very therapeutic utilization of those beatbox sounds. Hypnotic Beatboxing has a narrower field of sounds that it implements. The focus is more on basic percussive sounds.

Hypnotic Beatboxing uses a limited amount of sounds. It focuses primarily positive verbal formulas and basic beatbox sounds. It does not have to be limited to only a few sounds but can be enhanced as the user grows in sound making skills. For the sake of simplicity we will focus on only a few sounds in this book.

To learn more beatbox sounds you can check out any host of basic beatboxing tutorials on YouTube or www.humanbeatbox.com to further you skill level.

Influencing Others

Hypnotic Beatboxing is not limited to making your own life better. It can also be used as a tool to influence other people. While it is most commonly in an advertisement fashion it can be used in daily scenarios if done well.

In a conversation with someone you might be comfortable with, you could share this technique. This could help them with their stresses and challenges. In a workplace you could use this Hypnotic Beatboxing as a group encouragement and for morale.

While Hypnotic Beatboxing works best with those whom we are familiar with it. Hypnotic Beatboxing can be done suddenly through the advertisement medium. An example of this would be recording yourself (recording and looping discussed in a later section)) and playing it in the background of your home.

Having this ambient background track with or without a hypnotic beatbox formula, could ease the mood in the house. Also you could boost the morale of people around you. This is a way of creating a likeability and can enhance your relationships in the future.

As mentioned before it is important to remember the power of suggestibility. If you say something you can elicit a response or an emotion from somebody. This is important to capitalize on in order to make certain changes.

There are two techniques employed with Hypnotic beatboxing. First they are merely doing a beat in a hypnotic way. The second way is to do a beat in a formula of words with a positive affirmation. It is the second way that is most effective and potent. At this point it is only your voice and no instruments or recording. Recording and looping will be discussed later. In the voice only method there is an alternating word and beatbox sound similar the diagram below

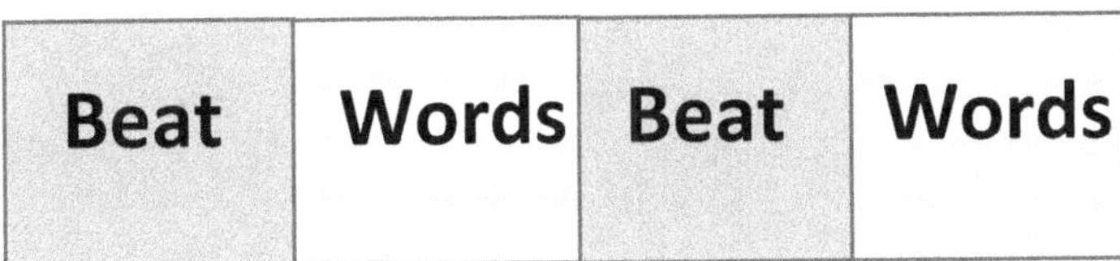

Beat	Words	Beat	Words

tt   I   tt   **am happy.**

All **beats** and **words** come from the mouth only.

Stand alone sounds

Hypnotic Beatboxing can be formulas of words or phrases with beatbox sounds. It can also be just the sounds of beatboxing as you breathe in and out. Although this model is more traditional of Pneumoboxics breathing it has a hypnotic role as well. And examples are as follows.

Repeatedly doing sound and focusing solely on the sounds. It can be very relaxing and trance like. For example would be repeating the letter "t" aloud.

    t t t t

Shaker shshshsh

Hi- hat tttt

Bass Kick bbbb

Share kkkk

Put them between words is like beatboxing and singing at the same time, a respected beatbox technique. Formulas and patterns of more complexity enhance its therapeutic value. For now we will focus on the individual sounds of Hypnotic Beatboxing. It is important to note that these are not the only sounds you can use in Hypnotic Beatboxing. If you can make more sounds, you can use those sounds too.

In the next chapter we will cover some of the basic sounds that the Hypnotic Beatboxer can use.

THE SOUNDS WE USE

- As a beatboxer I have learned many sounds and techniques throughout the years. In 2007 I was staying with a friend from college in Iowa for Halloween. I was talking to his roommate who was a musician about my doubts in my abilities. He said "You work with what you have. If you only have a few sounds such as humming and a basic drums. You can work with that and build from there." Since then I have grown vastly in my beatboxing and musican skills. But that advice was encouraging. The moral of this story is that you only need a few moves (Sounds).

- In this section we will discuss basic sounds used in Hypnotic Beatboxing patterns or formulas. This is just a short list of sounds you can use for this therapy.

Since this form of hypnosis uses "beatboxing" sounds it can implement many sounds. For simplicity we will stick to the simplest of sounds and a short list of them. If you wish to explore more sounds to make you can find scores of tutorials on Youtube or the internet by searching "how to beatbox". In Hypnotic Beatboxing we use not only singular sounds, but also combinations of sounds to gain the benefit it gives. Also important to note, is that we use powerful phrases in combination with these "beatbox sounds.

The breakdown of the following the sounds will include.

- **The sound**
- **The representative lettering for writing your own formulas**
- **A picture tutorial**
- **Simple patterns**
- **A scenario of its usage**

Bass Kick (b)

The Bass Kick is a base drum sound used in beatboxing and drum rhythms. The representative lettering is or "b".

Say the word "big" but without the "ig". Tighten your lips and breathe out. A letter *b* trying to keep your lips tight.

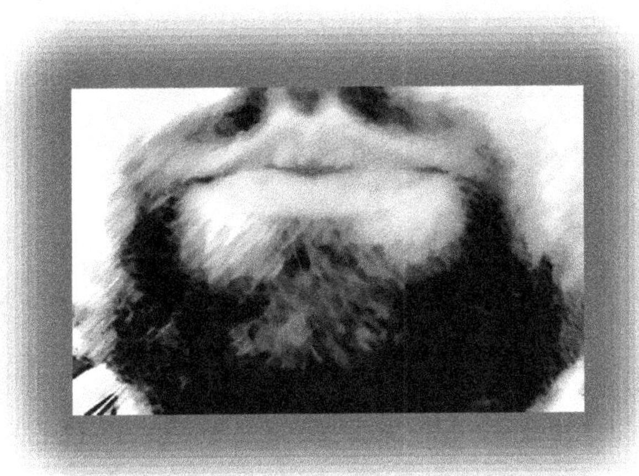

- Breathe in first.

- **bb** | **bb** am **bb** fine.

- Breathe out a stream of four to eight "b's":

b b b b | **b b b b** am **b b b b** fine **b b b b.**

b

"Breathe in. Breathe out.
Breathe in. Breathe out."

Bass Kick Application Example

Negative thought or feeling your having: "I have failed at something more than once. I will never get it right."

Instead of trying to fight the feeling of failure and why you can not do something correctly, take a deep breath in and hold for a moment. Next breathe out a bass kick pattern. Try four to eight "b's": b b b b. Focus on the sound your mouth makes when you do the bass kick pattern.

Snare (k)

The Snare is punctuating sharp sound used in beatboxing and drum rhythms. The representative lettering is "k".

Breathe out a letter *k* as in the word "kid". Blow out as you make your "k" sound.

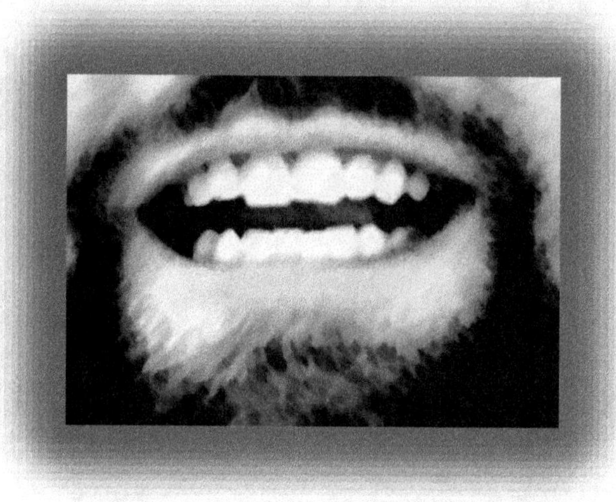

Snare Patterns

- Breathe in first.

- **kk** I **kk** am **kk** fine **kk**.

- Breathe out a steady stream of "k's". Try four "k's":

  k k k k I **k k k k** am **k k k k** fine **k k k k**.

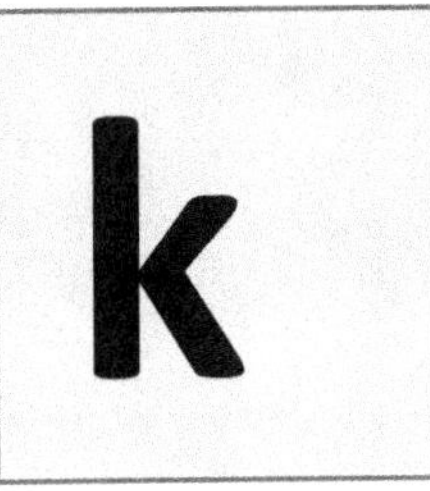

Snare Application Example

Negative thought or feeling your having: "It hurts my feelings when people are rude."

Instead of trying to fight the feeling of being disrespected or insulted, take a deep breath in and hold for a moment. Next breathe out a snare pattern. Try four to eight "k's": k k k k. Focus on the sound your mouth makes when you do the Snare pattern.

Hi-hat (t) or "tk"

The Hi-hat is a cymbal-like sound used in beatboxing and drum rhythms. The representative lettering is "t" or "tk".

A Hi-hat is saying the letter" t" just like sounding out the word "tiger". But instead of saying the full word "tiger", you only do the "t". You omit the "iger". For faster rhythms say "ticka ticka", rapidly, one after another. (tk)

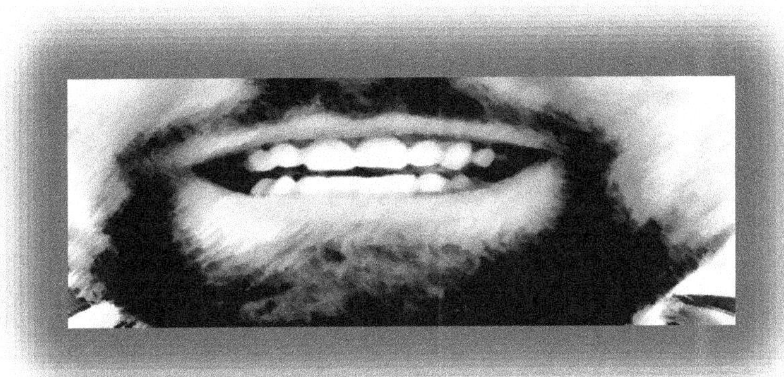

Hi-hat Patterns (t) (tk)

- Take a deep breath in first.

- **tt** I **tt** am **tt** fine **tt** (**tk tk** I **tk tk** am **tk tk** fine **tk tk**.

  t t t t I **t t t t** am **t t t t** fine **t t t t**.

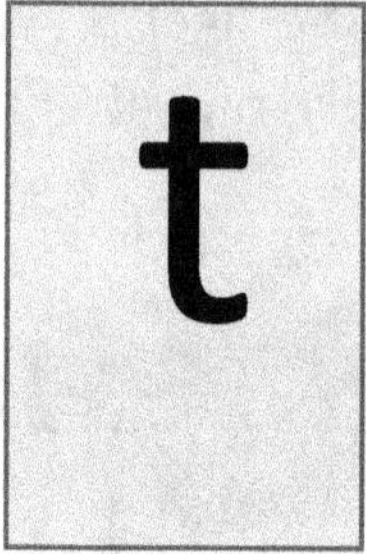

Inhale (i)

The inhalation sound is basically a dramatic inhalation sound. It is a punctuating sharp sound used in beatboxing and drum rhythms. The inhale sound can be a catchy way to "catch your breath" in the middle of a complex or lengthy drum pattern. The inhalation sound is not as widely used as other beatbox sounds. A cool thing about this sound is that it is very natural and anyone who breathes does it already. That is *everyone*. So much for the excuse many people say "I can't do that. I am not a beatboxer." Yes, you are. (Laughter) The representative lettering is "i".

- Breathe out first.
- Breathe in short separate breaths until your lungs are full of air.
- Simply do dramatic inhalation sounds like a *sigh*.
- Resume normal breathing at the end of a rythym.

It helps to keep in mind the direct association this sound has with breathing.

Inhale Patterns

- This method is all breathing but in short and separate breaths.

- Try four partial separate inhalations.

- I I am i fine i.

Note: Make your exhalation sound short between each word so you do not run out of breath. If you do run out of breath take a short breath in after couple words, or halfway through the pattern.

"Feel that rich oxygen fill your lungs."

Negative thought or feeling your having: "I feel upset. . ."

Instead of trying to fight the feeling of being upset or being bothered trying to fix what is causing the issue, let your breath out this time but to a relaxing point. Than breathe a short separate breaths pattern. Try i i i i. Focus on the dramatic sigh-like sound your mouth makes when you do the inhale pattern.

Shaker (sh)

The Shaker is a light rattling sound similar to a mother trying to soothe her infant. The Shaker can also be adapted to sound like white noise, which is very relaxing to many people. The Shaker can be used in place of the Hi-hat in beatbox and drum rhythms. The representative lettering is "sh".

Say "shh" like telling someone to be quiet. Say "sh" separately and repeatedly to create the breathing rhythm. "sh sh sh sh sh".

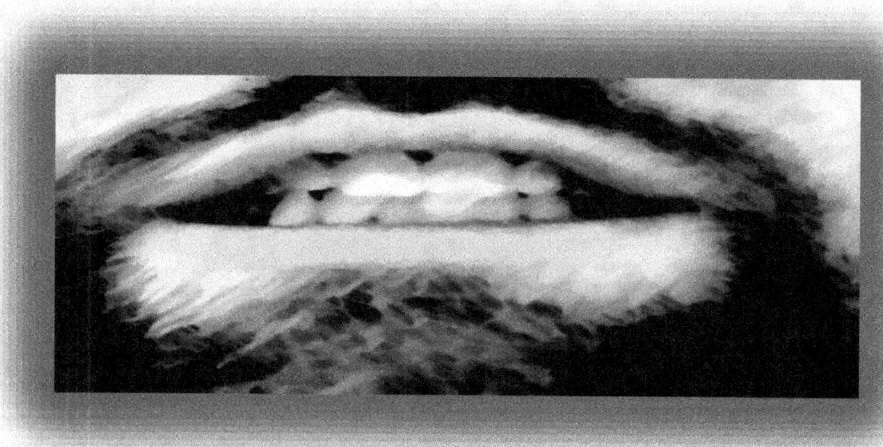

Shaker Patterns

- Take a deep breath in first.

- **sh sh** I **sh sh** am **sh sh** fine **sh sh**.

   sh sh sh sh I **sh sh sh sh** am **sh sh sh sh** fine **sh sh sh sh**.

sh

"Breathe slowly. Breathe Deliberately."

Shaker Application Example

Negative thought or feeling your having: "I feel worried. "

Instead of trying to fight the feeling or thoughts of worry. Take a deep slow breath and breathe out a Shaker pattern. Try four to eight separate "sh's": sh sh sh sh. Focus on the sound your mouth makes when you do the Shaker pattern.

Whistling (whr)

Whistling is an intersection of three different therapeutic Beatboxing techniques; *The Pneumoboxics Breathing Technique, The Bioboxics Breathing Technique*, and Hypnotic Beatboxing. Whistling a simple single note or two for a short time can be relaxing and distract you from something that maybe stressful. You can use your whistle by matching a pitch of a bird and focus on the sound the bird makes. Pick one bird. Listen to that bird. Whistle to match the pitch. Listen to your whistle as you do it. Do not worry about perfect sound or pitch. Focus on the sounds of you and the bird. First you take a full slow breath inward and blow out a whistle as a rhythm. The representative lettering is "whr".

Whistling can be simple, single note rhythms, or it can be complex patterns of melodies. It can be musical or even tuneless. Whatever sounds you are comfortable with doing is okay.

How to Whistle.

1. Wet your lips by licking them.

2. Place your lips in the shape of an *o* exposing your upper front teeth.

3. Place your tongue behind your two front teeth while touching the roof of your mouth slightly, (you can even have a gap between the roof of your mouth and your tongue.)

4. Blow out a nice, steady stream of air while maintaining the *o* lip position.

5. To change the pitch you can move your tongue around. You can also move your lips around. Make adjustments accordingly as you listen to the whistle's pitch and note.

Whistle- Whistle Whistle-whistle

Chose a couple notes.

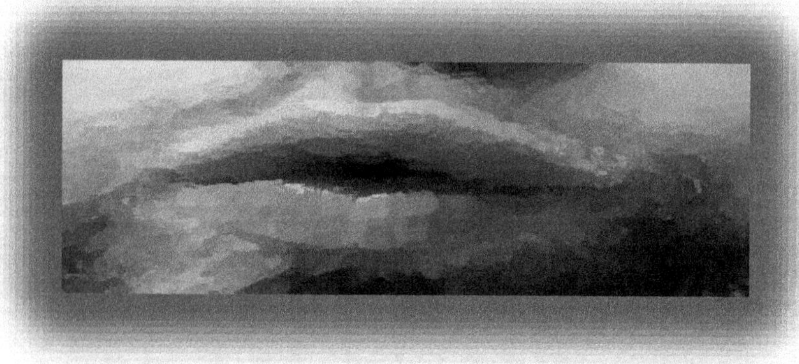

- Breathe in first.

- Breathe out four separate whistles of any single note. whr whr whr whr

- whrwhr whrwhr

- Breathe a whistle out for the count of four or eight if you can.

- Breathe out a single note until you are out of breath. Resume normal breathing.

- **Whr I Whr Am Whr fine Whr.**

whr (1 2 3 4)

whr (1 2 3 4 5 6 7 8)

Natural Sounds

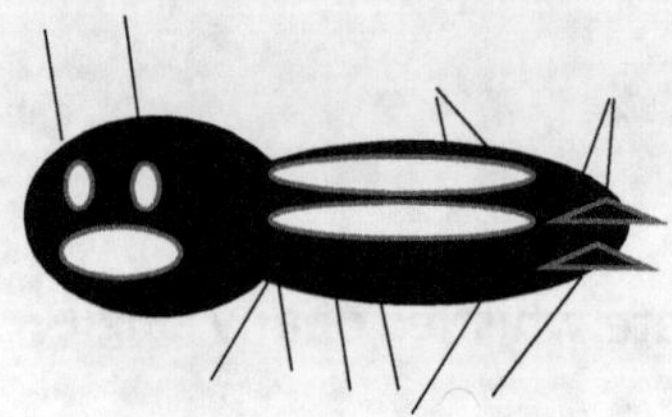

Natural sounds can be used in combination with a bass kick, hi hat, snare, or any basic percussive sound. Some of these sounds can be a heartbeat (throat kick) inhalation or exhalation, birds and crickets, oceanic sounds. Natural sounds such as a wind-like sound can be very effective in creating ambient moods for Hypnotic Beatboxing formulas.

Heartbeat Sound

1. Make is a swallowing motion with your throat.
2. Say "ug".
3. Keep your "ug" short and punchy.
4. This requires little air.
5. Do two separate "ugs" at a time to create a heartbeat rhythm. **ug ug   ug ug**

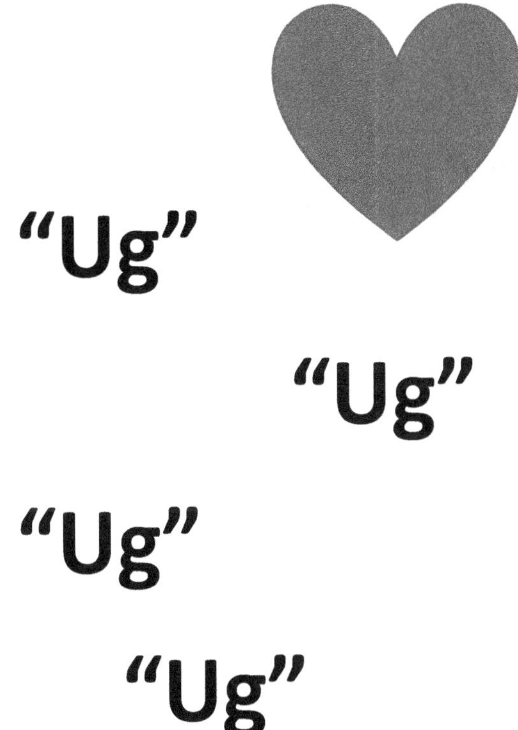

"Ug"

"Ug"

"Ug"

"Ug"

Wind Blowing

1. Place your lips in the shape of an "o".
2. Curve your tongue upward towards the roof of your mouth.
3. Blow out a steady stream of air.
4. Move your lips outward and inward or up and down but do not close your mouth completely.
5. For intensity adjust the amount of air that you blow out.

"Woorr"

1. Place your lips in the shape of an "o" after wetting them.
2. Curve your tongue behind your teeth to just about touching your teeth.
3. With your mouth and your tongue in this position blow out steady bursts of air.

Note: The cricket sound is a form of whistle.

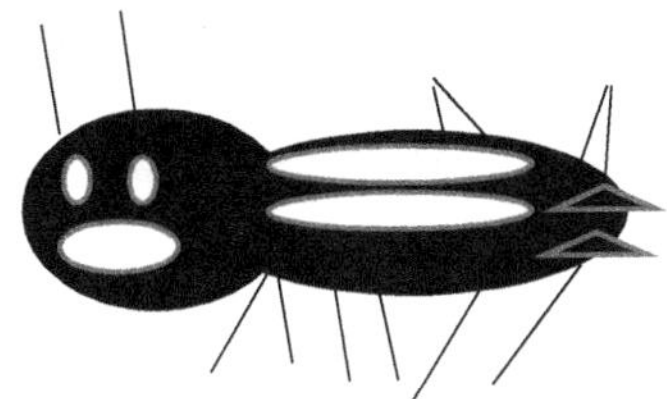

"Chirp"

"Chirp"

"Chirp"

Oceanic and Wind Sounds

The sound of the ocean or a gentle breezy stream of air from the mouth. It can be very effective for creating a calm or a mood for change. It is very similar to the wind sound.

1. Open your mouth and place your tongue in a curved upright position towards the roof of your mouth.
2. Breathe out gently a "shooor". Move your lips in and out and up and down as you breathe out and breathe in gently.
3. The sound that resembles the air of the ocean and your mouth are very similar modes. They are natural air.

"Shooor"

HYPNOTIC BEATBOXING
PHRASE PATTERNS

Hypnotic Beatboxing Patterns

- While working on this book I was originally utilizing long formulas similar to traditional hypnotic formulas. I had a realization that they may be difficult to implement so I revised them. For the sake of ease I shortened the formulas and patterns to be quicker and easier to implement.
- In this section we will discuss using beatboxing pattens and formulas to get physical and mental health benefits. Also we will discuss techniques for applying these patterns.

Definition: A Hypnotic Beatboxing pattern *is a sequence of beatbox sounds and positive words in a sentence structure.* Hypnotic Beatboxing patterns are short and easy to remember and to cite.

Hypnotic Beatboxing is customizable, and you can use whatever phrase you wish to use. Positive phrases work best. First you take a breath inward. Then you breathe out the pattern. In the shorthand it is effective and easy to think of Hypnotic Beatboxing like sentences between each word or phrase.

Hypnotic Beatboxing patterns are not as lengthy or complex as a complete Hypnotic Beatboxing formula. They are meant to be able to be delivered to oneself while out and about and to achieve deep relaxation. The kind of relaxation that you can get in the middle of the day may be different than laying in your bed and relaxing to a

Hypnotic Beatboxing audio. Patterns are more for quick relaxation, or relief. Formulas are for programming change in your life for the better.

tt I **kk** am **bb** calm **tt**. Yes **tt** I am.

tt I **kk** can **tt** do this **kk**. Yes **tt** I can.

bb One **bb,** two **tt,** three **kk,** four **bb.**

t I **t** will **t** win **t.**

tt I **tt** am **tt** ok **tt.**

bb I **kk** am **bb** fine **bk.**

tt I **tt** am **tt** fine **tt.**

kk I **kk** will **kk** be okay **kk.**

tt I **kk** am good **tt** at___________ **kk.**

shsh I **shsh** am **shsh** relaxed **shsh.**

bb I **bb** will **bb**________ **bb.**

tt k tt k tt

b t k t b t k t

sh sh sh sh

tttt

bt I **bt** did **bt** well **bt.**

tt I **tt** can **tt** change **tt.**

shsh I **shsh** am **shsh** happy.

bb I **bb** am **bb** peaceful **bk.**

bb You are calm **bb** and relaxed **bb**, as you breathe **bb** in, and breathe out **bb**.

The 20 Second Rule

For a number of these short patterns you can treat them as 20 seconds long. For example we will break down the following hypnotic beatboxing phrase.

t l **tt** am **tt** fine.

One sound and one short word equals one count. In this short phrase there are four counts. Doing the phrase five times would equal approximately 20 seconds worth of this exercise.

    t l **tt** am **tt** fine.

    1   **2**   **3**   **4**

If you feel like you can count to 20 and your head go ahead and do so while doing this pattern or any number of these patterns to follow. If it is difficult for you to maintain your focus you can set a stopwatch on most any cell phone or tablet. You let it run and watch it count to 20 as you do the pattern. This can also help you keep in time. While keeping in time is not necessary it can be beneficial. Once you have completed a cycle of 20 seconds you can continue. It is my theory, based off of a circulatory system cycle in the average human body takes 120 seconds that if you were to do six of these cycles it gives your body a full cycle worth of blood flow and breathing to calm down or relax.   Regardless of whether science is on the side of this argument, it could be beneficial to just relax for a minute and 120 seconds or 2 minutes.

Hand Washing

Another useful trick that you could employ while doing these patterns is to do them while washing your hands.

Hand washing is a necessity to get rid of bad things on your hands. It takes a little bit of time to be thorough so why not multi-task with a Hypnotic Beatboxing formula. The English alphabet is about 20 seconds long or so doing the Hypnotic Beatboxing pattern five times while washing your hands and having the circular motion of your hands lathering and repeating and rinsing can reinforce the mindfulness of this exercise.

"tt I tt am tt fine."

Phrase Patterns

In Hypnotic Beatboxing short beatbox patterns accompany short phrases. These are phrase patterns. These can be done anywhere and anytime. They do not require a lot of expertice. With a few times practicing these breathing phrase patterns you can benefit from them. Remember that these phrase patterns are to be done slowly. They use breath and a steady pace.

Hypnotic Beatboxing-Hi-Hat (Phrase Pattern)

Breathe in for four seconds.

Breathe out a pattern.

tt I **tt** am **tt** okay **tt**.

Repeat.

Hypnotic Beatboxing-Hi-Hat (Phrase Pattern)

Breathe in for four seconds.

Breathe out a pattern.

tt I **tt** am **tt** calm **tt**.

Repeat.

Hypnotic Beatboxing-Hi-Hat (Phrase Pattern)

Breathe in for four seconds.

Breathe out a pattern.

tt I **tt** am **tt** retaxed **tt**.

Repeat.

Hypnotic Beatboxing-Hi-Hat (Phrase Pattern)

Breathe in for four seconds.

Breathe out a pattern.

tt I **tt** am **tt** happy **tt**.

Repeat.

Hypnotic Beatboxing-Bass Kick/Hi-Hat (Phrase Pattern)

Breathe in for four seconds.

Breathe out a pattern.

 bb I **tt** am **bb** fine **tt**.

Repeat.

Hypnotic Beatboxing-Bass Kick (Phrase Pattern)

Breathe in for four seconds.

Breathe out a pattern.

bb I **bb** am **bb** fine **bb**.

Repeat.

Hypnotic Beatboxing-Bass Kick (Phrase Pattern)

Breathe in for four seconds.

Breathe out a pattern.

bb I **bb** am **bb** okay **bb**.

Repeat.

Hypnotic Beatboxing-Bass Kick (Phrase Pattern)

Breathe in for four seconds.

Breathe out a pattern.

bb I **bb** am **bb** peaceful **bb**.

Repeat.

Hypnotic Beatboxing-Full Drum (Phrase Pattern)

Breathe in for four seconds.

Breathe out a pattern.

bbl tt am **kk** happy **tt.**

Repeat.

Hypnotic Beatboxing-Full Drum (Phrase Pattern)

Breathe in for four seconds.

Breathe out a pattern.

b t l **k t** am **b t** happy **k t**.

Repeat.

Hypnotic Beatboxing-Full Drum (Phrase Pattern)

Breathe in for four seconds.

Breathe out a pattern.

b t k t I **t k t** am **b k t** fine **t k t**.

b t k t I **t k t** will **b k t** be alright **t k t**.

Repeat.

Hypnotic Beatboxing-Heartbeat Breath (Phrase Pattern)

Breathe in for four seconds.

Breathe out a pattern.

 ug ug I (*inhale* **i**) am **ug ug** fine (*exhale* **e**).

ug ug I (*inhale* **i**) will **ug ug** be alright (*exhale* **e**).

Repeat.

Hypnotic Beatboxing-Heartbeat Breath (Phrase Pattern)

Breathe in for four seconds.

Breathe out a pattern.

ug ug I (*inhale* **i**) am **ug ug** calm (*exhale* **e**).

ug ug and relaxed (*inhale* **i**) I will **ug ug** be alright (*exhale* **e**).

Repeat.

Hypnotic Beatboxing-Full Drum (Phrase Pattern)

Breathe in for four seconds.

Breathe out a pattern.

b t k t I **t k t** am **b k t** doing **t k t**.

b t k t a **t k t** good **b k t** job **t k t**.

Repeat.

Hypnotic Beatboxing-Hi-Hat Breath (Phrase Pattern)

Breathe in for four seconds.

Breathe out a pattern.

tt l l tt e am **tt i** fine **tt e.**

Repeat.

Hypnotic Beatboxing-Snare Breath (Phrase Pattern)

74

Breathe in for four seconds.

Breathe out a pattern.

kk i I **kk e** am **kk i** fine **kk e.**

Repeat.

Hypnotic Beatboxing-Snare (Phrase Pattern)

Breathe in for four seconds.

Breathe out a pattern.

 kk I **kk** will **kk** be okay **kk.**

Repeat.

Hypnotic Beatboxing-Shaker Breath (Phrase Pattern)

Breathe in for four seconds.

Breathe out a pattern.

sh sh i l **tt e** am **sh sh i** fine **sh sh e.**

Repeat.

Hypnotic Beatboxing-Shaker Exhale (Phrase Pattern)

Breathe in for four seconds.

Breathe out a pattern.

sh sh i I **sh sh e** am **sh sh i** happy **sh sh e.**

Repeat.

Hypnotic Beatboxing-Fill in the Blank (Phrase Pattern)

Breathe in for four seconds.

Breathe out a pattern.

sh sh i I sh sh e am sh sh i _______ sh sh e.

sh sh i I sh sh e______ sh sh i _____sh sh e

Repeat.

Hypnotic Beatboxing-Fill in the Blank (Phrase Pattern)

Breathe in for four seconds.

Breathe out a pattern.

 b t k t I **t k t** am **b k t** doing ______**t k t** and

b t k t k t_____ life **b k t** will **t k** t_____.

Repeat.

PHRASE PATTERN FORMULAS

- While I figured that short formulas were beneficial for positive affirmations more was needed for Hypnotic Beatboxing. Despite the formulas of traditional Hypnotic Beatboxing being longer and more in depth they can be difficult to practice. In conjunction with Hypnotic Beatboxing of long formulas could more difficult to incorporate with extra percussion. I wanted to make it simpler and remain effective. I shortened the formulas to more paragraph-like.

- In this section we will look at some basic, easy to implement formulas and patterns. We will cover some of the phyisical and mental health challenges addressed by these formulas.

Phrase Pattern Formulas

Sometimes the goals we may have are more than dealing with immenent moods or feelings such as anxiety or stress. These situations or problematic mindframes can take the form of lifestyle and addiction. More specifically this deals with things such as addictions, motivation, or deepening your relaxation further. Perhaps you struggle with motivation. In Hypnotic Beatboxing phrase pattern formulas are longer that a simple phrase pattern. They have more command for change and more sounds. A typical hypnotic formula can be over twenty minutes or longer. With Hypnotic Beatboxing phrase patterns, they are desingned to work quickly. They act as a reinforcement of a good mindset or behaviour. They interupt a negative thought pattern: "I want a cigarette!" is replaced with a quick and powerful formua to fight the craving. These formulas are designed to be quick and easy to deliver. You can use regular hypnotic or Hypnotic Beatboxing formulas for further reinforcement if you wish. In the appendixes there are more complex patterns. For now we will stick to two-the Hi-hat and the Shaker. Patterns and phrases to follow are topical and confront the various issues we face emotionally, in life style, and addictions. This is where Hynotic Beatboxing gains its real traction.

Relaxation and hypnosis or Hypnotic Beatboxing go hand in hand. The following formula can help you kick back and relax. It is short and simple, just what you need to get into relaxation.

Relaxation-Hi-hat (Formula Pattern)

Breathe in for four seconds.

tt I am calm **tt**

tt and relaxed. I go deeper **tt** and deeper into relaxation.

tt I am peaceful, loose, limp, **tt** and relaxed.

tt I go deeper and deeper into peacefulness. **tt** I am comfortable.

tt I am peaceful **tt** and relaxed.

tt I let go of my thoughts and feelings **tt** and embrace peace and relaxation.

Repeat.

Relaxation-Shaker (Formula Pattern)

Breathe in for four seconds.

shsh I am calm **shsh**

shsh and relaxed. I go deeper **shsh** and deeper into relaxation.

shsh I am peaceful, loose, limp, **shsh** and relaxed.

shsh I go deeper and deeper into peacefulness. **shsh** I am comfortable.

shsh I am peaceful **shsh** and relaxed.

shsh I let go of my thoughts and feelings **shsh** and embrace peace and relaxation.

Repeat.

Quitting Smoking

For the example of addictions one of the most common is nicotine or tobacco. Hypnosis long has been associated with smoking cessation. Whether you want to quit all together or just cut back hypnosis can help. Hypnotic Beatboxing uses a beat or soundscapes along with an empowering and relaxing formula. These short formulas or phrases, can be used in a time of imminent need, such as the time of a craving. I have found that the power of Hypnotic Beatboxing is threefold. First it uses a beat. The beat is potent and distracting and requires focus. Second is breathing as natural, empowering and healing. Breathing is something that you need to do. One of the main things about smoking is that it requires breathing in and breathing out. The third is a potent change formula. This three-fold technique is lethal against problems of the mind. It is a very effective tool. It is compact and deliverable.

Quitting Smoking-Hi-hat (Formula Pattern)

Breathe in for four seconds.

tt I have enough **tt.**

tt I am **tt** complete.

tt I can live **tt**

tt a life without smoking **tt**.

tt I enjoy **tt**

tt the benefits of a healthy **tt** lifestyle.

Repeat.

Quitting Smoking-Shaker (Formula Pattern)

Breathe in for four seconds.

shsh I have enough **shsh.**

shsh I am **shsh** complete.

shsh I can live **shsh**

shsh a life without smoking **shsh.**

shsh I enjoy **tt**

shsh the benefits of a healthy **shsh** lifestyle.

Repeat.

Coping with Anger

Anger can be dangerous. It is an indicator of something deeper going on in your life. It can be a very strong emotion and if left unchecked it can have devastating effects. In Hypnotic Beatboxing there are strong powerful and relaxing formulas that are quick to cite and do and are calming. They are also designed to help you delve in the process of coping and bettter dealing with situations that cause anger.

Coping with Anger-Hi-hat (Formula Pattern)

Breathe in for four seconds.

 tt I am calm, **tt**

tt relaxed, **tt** and peaceful.

tt I can deal with stresses **tt**

tt and confrontations and remain in control of my

emotions **tt**.

tt I can feel my emotions **tt**.

tt and accept what I can control and what I can not control

tt I am calm, **tt** relaxed and peaceful.

Repeat.

Coping with Anger-Shaker (Formula Pattern)

Breathe in for four seconds.

shsh I am calm, **shsh**

shsh relaxed, **shsh** and peaceful.

shsh I can deal with stresses **shsh**

shsh and confrontations and remain in control of my

emotions **shsh**.

shsh I can feel my emotions **shsh.**

shsh and accept what I can control and what I can not

control **shsh** I am calm, **shsh** relaxed and peaceful.

Repeat.

Harm Reduction

Harm reduction is somewhat of a controversial approach to dealing with addiction. In harm reduction one aims to reduce their usage of substances or their access to harmful substances and methods of aquiring them. Mainstream recovery suggests complete abstinence. Harm reduction ultimately should have the goal of abstinence, but people are likely to fail if they set the goal too high. The idea that you can be perfect is unrealistic. Almost everybody knows that you should not use substances that will harm you. How to refrain from using them is the real topic of debate. At the core of harm reduction is the act of being disciplined. It is a practice in self- control. Just as you would not run a marathon by just having a will of mind and saying "I'm going to run a marathon". You break that Marathon down into steps and start jogging and building up your endurance. Then after long practice you were able to run the full Marathon. Another example is losing a lot of weight. Imagine you have fifty pounds of wieght to lose. You do not just lose it immediately. You have to strip away calories from you diet and exercise more. It is often easier for some people to cut back on a substance than to give it up all together. If you are in a situation where you are immediately danger, please seek help. If you think that harm reduction could be a way to cut back on a substance and hopefully be free of it someday, then the following technique can help you.

Harm Reduction-Hi-hat (Formula Pattern)

Breathe in for four seconds

tt I have enough **tt.**

tt I am **tt** complete.

tt I can choose **tt**

tt to say no or to say yes **tt** to substances and **tt** the amounts I use.

tt I can reduce my using easily **tt.**

tt I enjoy my ability to say yes or no **tt** and to cut back **tt** and be healthier.

Repeat.

Harm Reduction-Shaker (Formula Pattern)

Breathe in for four seconds

 shsh I have enough **shsh.**

shsh I am **shsh** complete.

shsh I can choose **shsh**

shsh to say no or to say yes **shsh** to substances and **tt** the amounts I use.

shsh I can reduce my using easily **shsh.**

shsh I enjoy my ability to say yes or no **shsh** and to cut back **shsh** and be healthier.

Repeat.

Coping with Stress

Stress is dealing with life and feelings of things that we have to do that may be difficult. Stress is more of an inward manifestation of an outward situation or problem. Stress can take a toll on a person physically and mentally. Hypnotic beatboxing uses powerful relaxation phrases of affirmation to abet a stress. Do this repeatedly until you feel relief from your stress. And do it often to continue to be stress-free.

Coping with Stress-Hi-hat (Formula Pattern)

Breathe in for four seconds.

tt I am calm **tt** and relaxed.

tt I can handle any stresses and challenges **tt** in life.

tt I am complete **tt** and strong.

tt nothing is to difficult to overcome **tt**.

tt I can be calm **tt** and relaxed,

tt even when life is difficult **tt**.

Repeat.

Coping with Stress-Shaker (Formula Pattern)

Breathe in for four seconds.

shsh I am calm **tt** and relaxed.

shsh I can handle any stresses and challenges **shsh** in life.

shsh I am complete **shsh** and strong.

shsh nothing is to difficult to overcome **shsh**.

shsh I can be calm **shsh** and relaxed**,**

shsh even when life is difficult **shsh.**

Repeat.

Coping with Anxiety

Anxiety, worry, and fear can be barriers to living a fulfilled life. Anxiety is at best a little bit of a nuisance. At worst it can be serious enough to interfere with daily living. Anxiety needs to be taken seriously. There are many coping skills and medicines people can take to deal with chronic debilitating anxiety. Hypnotic Beatboxing takes a distracting and mindful approach to coping with anxiety. This is also coupled with powerful phrase affirmations.

Coping with Anxiety-Hi-hat (Formula Pattern)

Breathe in for four seconds.

tt I am calm **tt**.

tt I am **tt** confident.

tt I can handle **tt** any fear.

tt I am strong. **tt** I am good **tt**. I am comfortable.

tt I am peaceful **tt**.

tt I can handle all things **tt**.

Repeat.

Coping with Anxiety-Shaker (Formula Pattern)

Breathe in for four seconds.

shsh I am calm **shsh**.

shsh I am **shsh** confident.

shsh I can handle **shsh** any fear.

shsh I am strong. **shsh** I am good **shsh**. I am comfortable.

shsh I am peaceful **shsh**.

shsh I can handle all things **shsh.**

Repeat.

Coping with Depression

Depression can be debilitating and life-threatening. Being able to redirect yourself from a negative or depressed mind-frame is essential in living a well-balanced life. The Hypnotic Beatboxing formula for depression is designed to quickly redirect you to a more positive mindset.

Coping with Depression-Hi-hat

(Formula Pattern)

Breathe in for four seconds.

tt I am happy **tt**.

tt I am **tt** more than enough.

tt I am positive **tt** and complete.

tt I feel good and see hope **tt**

tt in each day. **tt** There is always potential for **tt** good in life.

tt I am happy and content **tt** in life.

Repeat.

Coping with Depression-Shaker

(Formula Shaker)

Breathe in for four seconds.

shsh I am happy **shsh**.

shsh I am **shsh** more than enough.

shsh I am positive **shsh** and complete.

shsh I feel good and see hope **shsh**

shsh in each day. **shsh** There is always potential for **shsh** good in life**.**

shsh I am happy and content **shsh** in life.

Repeat.

Eating Healthy

Eating healthy can be difficult, but it does not have to be. If you find that you enjoy something it makes it easier to do. These Hypnotic Heatboxing suggestions are powerful and motivating. Use them to empower you to make and continue making healthy dietary decisions.

Eating Healthy-Hi-Hat (Formula Pattern)

Breathe in for four seconds.

 tt I can eat **tt.**

tt healthy choices and portions **tt** of food.

tt I enjoy healthy foods **tt.**

tt healthy eating is a lifestyle I thoroughly **tt** enjoy.

tt I enjoy recieving **tt**

tt the benefits of a healthy **tt** lifestyle.

Repeat.

Eating Healthy-Shaker (Formula Pattern)

Breathe in for four seconds.

shsh I can eat **shsh.**

shsh healthy choices and portions **shsh** of food.

shsh I enjoy healthy foods **shsh.**

shsh healthy eating is a lifestyle I thoroughly **shsh** enjoy.

shsh I enjoy recieving **shsh**

shsh the benefits of a healthy **shsh** lifestyle.

Repeat.

Increasing Exercise

It goes without saying the exercises important. It is not always easy for people to get motivated to exercise despite knowing its benefits. Using Hypnotic Beatboxing can help motivate you to exercise. This is because it encourages the behavior of exercising its the benefits

Increasing Exercise-Hi-Hat (Formula Pattern)

Breathe in for four seconds.

tt I can be healthy **tt.**

tt Exercise can be fun **tt.** I am motivated to exercise.

tt Exercise is enjoyable **tt.** I enjoy the benefits **tt** of exercise.

tt healthy eating and I can do it easily **tt.**

tt I enjoy **tt**

tt the benefits of a healthy **tt** lifestyle.

Repeat.

Increasing Exercise-Shaker (Formula Pattern)

Breathe in for four seconds.

shsh I can be healthy **shsh.**

shsh Exercise can be fun **shsh.** I am motivated to exercise.

shsh Exercise is enjoyable **shsh.** I enjoy the benefits **shsh**
of exercise.

shsh healthy eating and I can do it easily **shsh.**

shsh I enjoy **shsh**

shsh the benefits of a healthy **shsh** lifestyle.

Repeat

Increasing Motivation

We all need that little push every once in awhile. That push can help us get things done and strive for change in our lives. Motivation is intrinsic meaning it comes from inside. You can boost your motivation by circulating your airflow. This gives you energy while using a Hypnotic Beatboxing formula.

Increasing Motivation-Hi-hat

(Formula Pattern)

Breathe in for four seconds

tt I have strength **tt.**

tt I have energy and drive **tt** to get things done.

tt I can follow through with things **tt**

tt and accomplish **tt** the things that are important to me **tt**.

tt I enjoy **tt**

tt the accomplishments of my **tt** hard work.

Repeat.

Increasing Motivation-Shaker

(Formula Pattern)

Breathe in for four seconds

shsh I have strength **shsh.**

shsh I have energy and drive **shsh** to get things done.

shsh I can follow through with things **shsh**

shsh and accomplish **shsh** the things that are important to me **shsh.**

shsh I enjoy **shsh**

shsh the accomplishments of my **shsh** hard work.

Repeat.

Reaching Goals

Whether it be losing weight, a family vacation, painting the back porch, or running a marathon, we all have goals. Reaching goals can be difficult, but it does not always have to be. Goals are to be broken down into steps that are achievable and measurable. Using Hypnotic Beatboxing can be effective in motivating you and helping you focus on reaching your goals. Goal reaching, and motivation formulas work hand in hand. They reinforce the desire you have for making positive changes in your life.

Reaching Goals-Hi-hat (Formula Pattern)

Breathe in for four seconds.

tt I am calm tt and relaxed.

tt I am focused tt and intent on getting things done.

tt I and prioritize effectively tt and zero in on any task.

tt I can be timely tt and accomplish all necessary tasks.

tt I can set and reach tt reach goals tt.

tt I am able to get things done tt No task is too difficult for me.

tt I can also share responsibilities with other people tt When it is necessary.

Repeat.

Reaching Goals-Shaker (Formula Pattern)

Breathe in for four seconds.

shsh I am calm **shsh** and relaxed.

shsh I am focused **shsh** and intent on getting things done.

shsh I and prioritize effectively **shsh** and zero in on any task.

shsh I can be timely **shsh** and accomplish all necessary tasks.

shsh I can set and reach **shsh** reach goals **shsh**.

shsh I am able to get things done **shsh** No task is too difficult for me.

shsh I can also share responsibilities with other people **shsh** When it is necessary.

Repeat.

Fill in the Blank

Hypnotic Beatboxing is most enjoyable, unique and beneficial when a person tailors their own formulas. In the following section there are the Hi-hat and Shaker basic fill in the blank formulas. You can put whatever words in the blank you desire. There are almost infinite ways you can write a Hypnotic Beatboxing formula. Formula writing based on your needs. For example, if you do not struggle with depression, or want to get more work done at home, you could benefit from a powerful customized organizational formula

Fill in the Blank-Hi-hat (Formula Pattern)

Breathe in for four seconds.

tt I am ______________ **tt.**

tt I relax. **tt** I go deeper **tt** and deeper.

tt I am ____________ loose, limp, **tt** and relaxed.

tt I ____________ and____________ **tt** I can

____________.

tt I am able to ____________**tt.**

tt I can____________ **tt** and ____________.

Repeat.

Fill in the Blank-Shaker (Formula Pattern)

Breathe in for four seconds.

shsh I am _____________ **shsh.**

shsh I relax. **shsh** I go deeper **shsh** and deeper.

shsh I am _____________ loose, limp, **shsh** and relaxed.

shsh I _____________ and_____________ **shsh** I can

_____________.

shsh I am able to _____________**shsh.**

shsh I can_____________ **shsh** and _____________.

Repeat.

WRITING AND RECORDING FORMULAS

- When I initially discovered that I could write my own hypnotic formulas I was elated. It was a game changer. I added a beatbox, a dynamic that had not yet been practiced.

- In this section we will edelve into writing and delivering effective and enjoyable Hypnotic Beatboxing formulas. We will eplore the various parts of a formula and how to successfully deliver a hypnotic beatboxing formula. Furthermore we will look at how to record your own original Hypnotic Beatboxing formulas, at your leisure and your pace.

Formulas have several parts similar to writing a story. They have a beginning a body and an ending. They are filled with powerful suggestions of relaxation and change.

Beginning

Every good hypnotic or Hypnotic Beatboxing formula has a introductory section. In this part of the formula the hypnotist or the recording says deeply calming and relaxing words. In Hypnotic Beatboxing it could start out with a drum sound or words. In the beginning of many of these formulas are strong suggestions about breathing "slow" and "deep". Breath regulation is a crucial part of an effective hypnotic or Hypnotic Beatboxing session.

Body

The body contains the majority of the formula. This has a
continued aspect of relaxation and in mildly authoritative
suggestions. These could be "You are no longer driven by
hunger but eat enough and easily are satisfied. You can
and will be able to easily make healthy food choices. This
will come naturally."

End

The end of a hypnotic or hypnotic beatboxing formula
closes out the session with positive reinforcement of the
first two sections. In the conclusion or end section of the
formula may continue a count up or down to alertness. Or
invite you to "sleep or be wide awake."

The Words We Choose

The words you choose in a Hypnotic Beatboxing formula
can make all the difference in your experience. You want
to use straightforward language that is empowering.
Speak in the present tense and the here and now. Use
change language which may be the opposite of the
negative things in your life. Words like "am" and "are"
increase the effectiveness of a Hypnotic Beatboxing
formula. Speak slowly and clearly, with a calm voice while
using spaces and pausess between each word or phrase.
A good rule to think of is to: read a sentence or word-
pause, for a moment or two and then move on. In
Hypnotic Heatboxing these pauses can be heartbeat,
percussive or biological sound. At times they may be

ambient backgrounds like oceanic sounds or air. It is even okay to just use silence. Slow phraseology and speaking are crucial for Hypnotic Beatboxing formula. The pace at which we speak them in a formula is as important as the wording.

Formulas can be done with or without beats. You can also say formulas to yourself or read them off if you cannot remember them. It is important to record a formula if you want to listen to it. You can also have someone read it to you or do it with the beats.

In Hypnotic Beatboxing you space words and phrases out. Writing out your formula and reading it or memorizing it is key to successful delivery of the formula. You can also type it on a device like a laptop, tablet or a phone and read it as you record it. You can also just say the formula to yourself. This where Hypnotic Beatboxing really shines. It can be a formula or a simple phrase. The basic rules are as follows:

1. Breathe in first and exhale the formula out.
2. Use simple words.
3. Use positive words
4. Speak slowly.
5. Pause between words. The pauses are where you put your beatbox sounds.
6. Repeat.
7. Reflect.
8. Reward.

1. Breathe in First and Exhale the Formula Out.

Taking a deep breath in first, is the primary place to start. After taking your breath in, you hold it for a moment. Next you breathe out the formula or beat and formula slowly.

2. Use Simple Words.

In life many things are best when done with simplicity. The utilization of simple words and phrases such as monosyllabic words like, "good" or "fine" are effective in Hypnotic Beatboxing formulas. Using short simple words keeps your mind in focus, allowing you to relax more.

3. Use Positive Words

It would be unhelpful to use negative language in a Hypnotic Beatboxing formula. It is very important to use positive affirmations to create positive changes in your mood and life. That is why the words that you select are very important.

4. Speak Slowy.

Speak the words in your formula slowly and directly. This allows you to think of each word as it is being repeated by your voice or recording. Speaking and doing the beat slowly makes it easier to employ your formulas.

5. Pause Between Words.

The pauses are where you put your beatbox sounds. Taking a pause helps you slow down and relax even more. Pauses can be between a beat, words and also at the end of a phrase when your breath is fully expelled.

6. Repeat.

Repetition is the key to learning, as well as getting better at things in life. Repeat the formula at least one or two times and up to as many times as you feel comfortable with doing. You can also do your formula or pattern for as much as your airflow allows.

7. Reflect

Reflecting on the sounds that you are doing and the words you are saying is important. But even more important is to focus on how you are feeling throughout the experience. If possible, hold off on focusing on your feelings during the beat. Reflect on them before and after you do the beat. This reflection should help you gauge how you feel in comparison to how you felt. There is a very mindful aspect of Hypnotic Beatboxing and it requires focus.

8. Reward

Reward yourself with a praise in your head. You can also acknowledge the good feelings you may be having as a positive reinforcement. This reward can be a mental note to yourself that you completed the formula.   It can be doing a dance or sharing the experience with others. I reward myself for these formulas being written or done, by going for a walk.

Recording

Looping technology gives us the ability to enhance our formulas vastly. With looping technology you are able to layer and adjust volumes of pre-recorded or live recordings of sounds. This enables you to create massive soundscapes of relaxing music. Furthermore you can add relaxing vocalizations or you can add relaxing formulas. Another added benefit of looping is that you can just sit back, relax and focus on the beat and formula.

Listening of recording playback can be done in various ways. Some of these are loop stations, Apps or computer software, cameras, and pocket recorders.

Loop stations

Loop stations are the first and foremost devices for replaying your music in a live scenario. They have another benefit. Loop stations are widely used amongst many musicians. Recording pure sounds on a hardware such as a loop station, can enable you to experiment with the beatboxing and sounds and formulas you make. You can record this onto your computer and further enhance or add formulas to it and put it on a CD if you are old school

and use these old discs. You also can make your looped
recordings into an MP3's. The utilization of loop station
Hypnotic Beatboxing in a live and intimate setting such as
a one-on-one could be used by therapists to create
ambient soundscapes for a hypnotherapeutic session. This
will require more training on the therapist's part but could
be very well worth it. I have worked with colleague
therapists on this potential project of Hypnotic Beatboxing

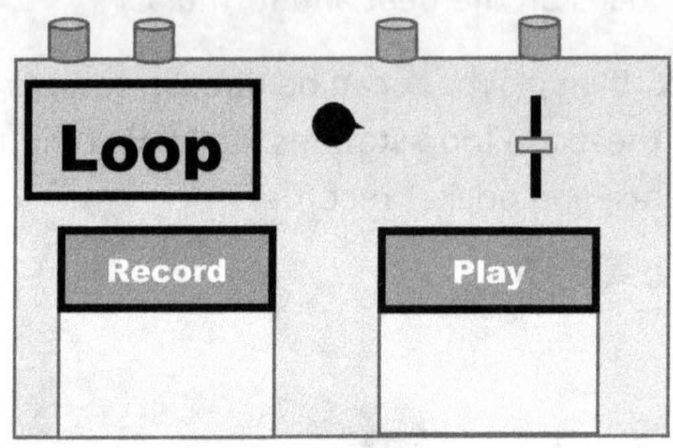

Apps or Computer Software

There are many apps that tablets and phones can use that
can record audio loops. The number of these apps enable
you to have multiple layers at a time. The primary focus of
many of these apps is musical, and some are already
designed for beatboxers. There could be a learning curve
for some of these Apps and softwares. As long as you
know a few sounds you can record them. In many of these
looping apps is the ability to replay what you have
recorded. Using earphones either Bluetooth or an auxiliary
input plug-in you can play your recordings and listen with

ease. You can also listen to the speaker of your phone or tablet.

There are hosts of musical software that can be employed on computers. A looping software can enable you to create very complex musical arrangements. I pioneered the genre Bioboxics, (an animal sounds based music genre made by human voice only). You can us animal sounds to create therapeutic soundscapes.

Using a Camera with Audio Playback

As long as a camera on a phone has a speaker to play the song back, it can be used for Hypnotic Beatboxing. Simply take your camera whether your phone, computer, tablet, and press record and do a single layer beat with a formula. This technique is only single layer unless you use a computer software or app to mix down multiple layers. It is a less than desirable technique for doing Hypnotic Beatboxing audio track for relaxation. It can work in a pinch. This can also serve to enhance your skills because you can watch yourself and learn from the visual. After you have recorded your formula, press play and listen with earphones or the speaker of your device.

Pocket Recorders

A pocket recorder is a device that you can use to record audio. Many of these devices allow you to record MP3 or wave sound formats. Pocket recorders are made in various different forms and can be either rechargeable or use batteries that you can replace. The nice thing about a pocket recorder is that you can carry it in your pocket for on-the-go recordings, hence the name "pocket". They are compact enough to take with you most anywhere. You do not have to have a fancy music studio to record yourself and your formulas.

Pocket recorders may be somewhat obsolete with the ability to use your phone for audio recording or tablets and computer technologymay have audio input to plug in extra devices. I have had several pocket recorders throughout the last decade. My current one uses a built-in USB plug-in to transfer files from the recorder to my computer. To use a pocket recorder you only need to be able to do a single formula. You can press record a play. If you have recorded five minutes worth of you doing a formula, you sit back and relax and listen for five minutes. If you worked it into a loop you can play it, for instance on my personal recorder has the ability for me to press play and hold and it will play a repeat the recording. Steps for recording are as follows.

1. Choose a recording device.

2. Decide a formula or a pattern to use. You can write your own formulas or you can use ones in this book.

3. Press record on the pocket recorder or recording device. (If you have a phone, you can download an app for recording. You can also open your camera function and press the video record button.)

4. Place your recorder device 6 to 12 inches away from your mouth so you can get good sound recording.

5. Do your beat and words clearly and slowly. Do not use too much airflow from your mouth as this can distort a recording.

6. Once you have finished recording your beat formula press stop.

 When you press stop or record you want to make sure not to be shaking the device or ruffling things near it because the device can pick up that background noise. This can distort the recording and make it distracting as you to listen to it.

7. Using the playback function on your device you can play your beat formula to listen and relax. It is best to find a relaxed place to do your recording and listening.

Editing

Recording and editing can be a thoroughly therapeutic and enjoyable technique to implement in recovery from stress and daily life. Recording and editing can be an investment but does not have to drain the wallet. You can use simple apps and software many of which are free to record your Hypnotic Beatboxing formula. There are some basics of recording and editing. You do not have to be a strong musician to do a decent recording. Simple is the best. In this section we will discuss some fundementals of recording. This can get you on your way to having a solid therapeutic Hypnotic Beatboxing formula in a time-sensitive fashion. Some of the basics are as follows:

- **Recording**
- **Imprting**
- **Looping**
- **Splitting or cutting and deleting**
- **Copy and paste**
- **Volume settings and mixing**
- **Panning**
- **Undo**
- **Range of recording and playback**
- **Rendering a file into an MP3**

There are many facets to recording. All you need is a few basic skills and techniques to get a good and usable recording. Once you have your initial recording it is only a few steps to having a beneficial and relaxing Hypnotic Beatbox formula that can be used over and over again.

Recording

To record, you use a microphone. Earphones are optional. You will need a computer, tablet, or phone with an app or software designed to record multiple audios. An individual audio would be one sound or take of recording. Think of the layers of the recording as if they were blocks stacked upon each other.

While recording a Hypnotic Beatbox formula, the layers are stacked and to get the right volume or clarity of a sound. When using a microphone you have to have proper placement. Microphone placement is how far you or your instrument are away from a mic when it is recording or in live play.

Importing

You may have a file recorded on an external device that has a USB capable transfer ability. To get this device's recording to or from a SD chip or USB thumb drive, you need to plug it into the computer. Computers often have a software to import files. You may want to insert an audio track or import or open that particular recording. The open icon is usually a folder or the word "Open" on the menu bar. You click select it and go into the desired folder that has the file that you want to use. Select it and then click ok to open the file.

Looping

The easiest way to think of looping is a sound that plays over and over. This sound can be in combination with other sounds to create a pattern or even a song. Much of modern music is loop-based. First you have to record your sound. Once you have recorded a particular sound you want to shave off the front and the end of that sound. Next copy and paste that same sound next to itself on the timeline of the software that you are using. Listen to the sound playing such as a cricket chirp repeating. If you record your cricket chirp shave off the ends by snipping with a little scissors icon tool. Delete the ends you copy and paste the original cricket sound next to the first cricket sound for as many as you desire. Once you have the first layer done you can add another by recording of another sound or rhythm. Volume adjustment is important for the loops in their individual placement.

Splitting or Cutting and Deleting

One of the things an old musician colleague of mine taught me is to record and keep the recording going. You do not have to stop every time untill you get a take that you like. Repeating the same sentence over and over and stumbling on it and that is okay. You can always edit errors out later. Splitting cutting and deleting usually have a scissors icon. Select your recording file. Where your cursor is will be the place that will get cut.   Another function may be to right click and there is a menu that says "split at cursor". When you split at cursor you can separate that part of the audio and remove a piece or make another split and remove a smaller piece. This technique is very useful in getting out things like extra breathing sounds when you take a breath in and do not want in a recording. This can be things like a verbalized pause like saying "um" or "ah", or just stumbling over words and not announcing them clearly. A simple comparison to this technique would be when you stencil something on paper with a pen or pencil and you take a scissors to cut off the excess. The excess is unusable or undesirable. With the cutting snipping or splitting functions undesired pieces can be removed from your recording. When you delete the snipped parts they are removed from the recording recording session to record my verbal formula as well as some extra sounds like a cricket trip a frog sound bird sound and ambient background sounds and drums. I usually do my verbal formula first and those sounds later I cut and paste those sounds clip them and then slide them down into other tracks to create my layers. This is a conservational tool to save time.

Copy and Paste

Copying and pasting is a very common thing to do while editing many documents on a computer or tablet. The process is very similar throughout each of these devices. You always want to select (usually this can be by right-clicking on the item you want to select) or if you are on a tablet holding down your finger until a menu comes up. This menu will give several options one of which is copy and the other is paste. For the sake of recording copying and pasting can act like looping. Once you have your item copied you go to the item you copied click next to it. Then right click untill you get the menu again. Select paste and you will have two of the same items next to each other. Listen to them to see if they are spaced out well enough and in tempo. You can repeat this process to have a full length of your recording worth of this sound. for example a cricket chirp *copied* and *pasted* next to another cricket chirp *pasted* next to a cricket trip.

"Chirp Chrip Chirp"

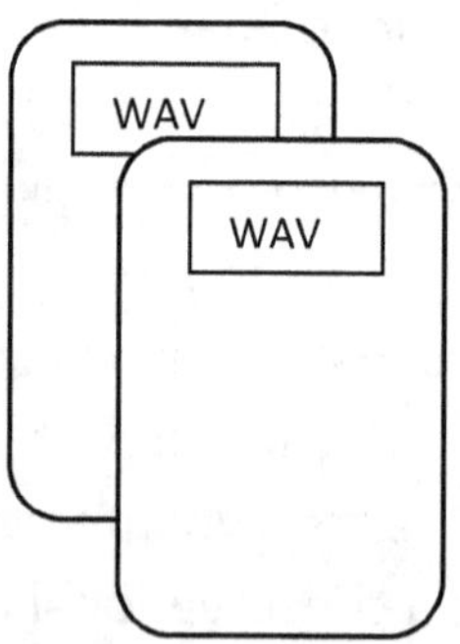

Volume Settings and Mixing

Volume is crucial in a decent recording. You need the proper amount of volume to be able to hear your recording with ease on any device or in earphones. Not all parts of the recording will have the same volume. It is for this reason that you mix each volume carefully in contrast to the other sound's volumes. For instance you have the chirp of a cricket. It has a particular volume. You have a cardinal tweeting sound. It has a particular volume. You also have a percussive sound such as a Bass Kick it has a volume finally. You have your words or formula recording and it has a separate volume. In this example you have four volumes to consider in contrast to each other. There is also a master volume over the entire recording. You want that to be your last adjustment. Most decent softwares have an equalizer that shows red when you are peaking. When the sound peaks it will be dissonant which is bad for a recording. This is true for the playback of the recording. You want to stay in the green on an equalizer (volume control). When a piece of sound is playing with it reads to a green and there is no red then you are recording will play back well. Each volume control will have this function. Your master volume control will also have this function. As a recording is playing you will hear individual sounds. If one sound is too loud, turn it down a little. Then relisten and if you notice that the sounds blend and you can hear them equally, procede to the next sound. If all parts are easily heard then you can be satisfied with the recording. The more layers you have the more complex and more micro adjustments to the volume you'll have to make. Within each of these single tracks of audio sound you can you can adjust the volume at different parts. The volume that is most important is the reading of the formula. That is the message and it should be a little louder than the "Beatbox" or ambient music. The message or formula of hypnosis is where the programing happens. Have it at a volume that you or others can clearly hear it and understand each word.

Panning

When you hear music through headphones or speaker plays from a left and a right side. The balance of the sound can be adjusted from left to right on an individual track. So if you have the cricket chirp, you can have it play through one earphone to the other. The sound can play through both at the same time. A panning or crossfading dial allows you to play it through the left or right side. In the balance you are able to do one side or the other or a spectrum of left to right. Using a panning effect can be quite useful in creating moods or feelings. You can also pan the vocal or the voice formula through one earphone to the next. You will want some balance. You do not want sound to constantly be playing left and right for a decent recording. This can be distracting if you have too much shuffling back and forth between your left and right ear. Panning can be a useful effect but should be done with discretion. If your earphones that are not the best they can it can make it difficult to hear the recording fully so you want balance.

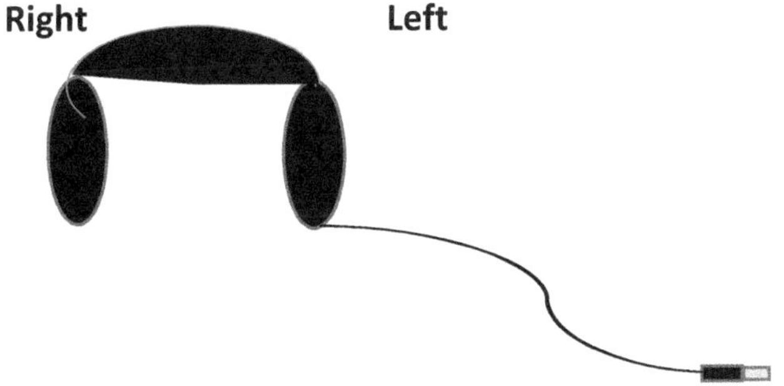

Undo

Definition: *undo is the function that allows you to reinsert or reapply something that is an error. This function allows you to return to a former state in your editing.*

The undo function can be a lifesaver if you made numerous errors and you want to get back to an original format. You can hit the undo button which is usually a backwards semi-circle arrow. The best way to record and edit is slow and thorough. The undo function can be useful in returning to something that you may want from your recording than what you currently have.

Range of Recording and Playback

Definition: *The range of your recording starts at the beginning or the intro of your recording to the very end of your recording.* The range can start before you have your recording start by sliding your recording over to the right. You can have it end of your recording as well. When you have your range selected and finalized you can export your file as an mp3. If you have a good range of playback where one sound blends into another you can engage the repeat function on your playing device. It can play seamlessly when it repeats. This can be very useful if you want to listen to your track over and over.

There are many forms of audio file that you can use. MP3 is the most usable across the board. Another famous format is a wav format

.

Rendering a File into an MP3

Many softwares have an export or rendering process to convert your software recording into a desirable format. These are often located in a toolbar, under a term such as *Edit* or *File*. You simply raise your cursor and hover or click on the *Edit* or *File* term at the top of the screen. This will bring down a menu in a box of different options rendering, converting or exporting are general terms you use. After you have selected the folder in which you save your mp3 in you hit OK. The export and the rendering process shall begin. It is important to have a good file saving system to make itl easier to locate your recordings. Always check the file's location to know where it is exported. A tip I use is to copy the finalized export of the MP3 into a music folder a specifically named folder for example "Hypnotic Beatboxing".

btkt btkt

sh sh sh sh sh

chewi chewi

i e i e i e i e

Woorr

You are calm and relaxed as you breathe in and hold for a moment. You breathe out and relax deeper.......

The diagram shows words or sounds stacked on top of each other. Your first layer that you record would be the "btkt." When you record again it would be the next layer which is a shaker the shaker *"sh."* Your third layer is your chewy scratch "chewi." Your fourth layer would be your inhalations and exhalation sounds or "I" and "e." Your fifth layer would be the wind sound or woorr. Your sixth layer is a Hypnotic Beatboxing formulas. It is easy to think of it like stacking blocks. All the blocks are in the same structure, but they are individual parts. Each of the sounds act as individual building blocks for a looped formula.

Note:

When you are using your camera to record audio you may not be trying to make a good video. This means when you listen to the recording afterwards it is not important to watch yourself on the camera. In fact it is best to just listen to the recording. You can do visual aspects to Hypnotic Beatboxing, but as for this topic, the focus is an audio recording.

Transferring Files

Transferring Hypnotic Beatboxing formulas via CD, MP3, wav, mp4 or other files can be beneficial for sharing with others. For personal use, take your recordings and you upload them to a built in media player on a computer and sync them to your desired devices.

Recording Mp3's or CDs

You can record your audio and put it onto a CD (compact disc) You can also make it into an MP3 file and put it onto a MP3 player or a phone and play it at your leisure.

Hypnotic Beatboxing can be used in passive muscle relaxation using bird and other nature all made by your voice.

As mentioned earlier, heart beats, wind, cricket and other natural sounds have an effect that can be very positive and relaxing in a formula.

Many different types of relaxation formulas will walk you through steps of relaxing various different muscles of the body. This often starts with the head and works down to the feet. These recordings frequently use ambient music and relaxing atmospheric sounds. Many of these formulas incorporate wildlife.

Combinations

You can do combinations of sounds to create more complex patterns. An example is as follows.

- Breathe in, hold for a moment.
- Breathe out animal sounds.

Pattern Example:

1. Cardinal-Robin-Dog (bark)- Cardinal-Robin-Dog (bark)
2. Repeat.

There is almost an infinite amounts of patterns you can do. You can also do a beatbox sound n your pattern.

Using Props or Visuals

With Hypnotic Beatboxing comes a mindful aspect. While you are listening to the formulas that you have recorded (or the recordings of other people) you can choose to either stare at some object. This will help you to zero in your attention and benefit the more from your relaxation. Do a Hypnotic Beatboxing formula and focus on a blade of grass or leaves on a tree. A prop could be holding something soft like a washcloth or a handkerchief and feeling it in your hands. These extra techniques can enhance the therapeutic value of your Hypnotic Beatboxing experience.

HYPNOTIC BEATBOXING AS A PROFESSION

- In my journey with Hypnotic Beatboxing I found it was to grand an idea or tool for wellness to just keep it to myself. Many people can benefit from it and possibly find a career doing Hypnotic Beatboxing. It is an overarching goal of mine to make hypnotic Beatboxing a potential career path for the future.
- In this section we will dig into the potential future of Hypnotic Beatboxing as it relates to career oportunities. We will also see barriers to this being a successful movement and steps to making it a profitable job.

The Jobs of a Hypnotic Beatboxer

Psychology has long stood as a field of science. Within that branch of science are many different therapies and occupations. This plainly means that people can be paid to help other people using techniques or therapies. This can be incorporated on a large scale, making particular jobs available. Let's look at some of the jobs to a Hypnotic Beatboxer.

The Jobs of a Hypnotic Beatboxer

Many people like to beatbox, but how about making it a job. Many people use hypnosis and like to give help to people through suggestion. The marriage of Beatboxing and hypnosis could prove to have several job potentials. Yes job potentials, and with that comes pay. Some of the potentail jobs Hypnotic Beatboxer are in the following areas.

- **Hypnotic beatboxing as a therapist or hypnotherapist**
- **Peer Support or Groups**
- **Lecturing**
- **Recording Hypnotic Beatboxing**
- **Video making of hypnotic beatboxing**
- **Training**
- **Formula Writing**
- **Research**

Hypnotic Beatboxing Therapist for Hypnotherapist

There are many people that need hypnotherapy. There is even a choice group of people to do the hypnotherapy. While you may be able to listen to audio from the web sometimes an in person encounter is more beneficial or necessary.

Peer Support or Groups

This is an area of much intrigue. Peer support in the mental health realm is a growing field. Many peers are able to be employed and offer insight and help in the mental health care field. In a Hypnotic Beatboxing field an opinion of a peer can be vast and its effect. A peer can offer insights on help with recovery from various different issues. Teaching this as a peer could be very advantageous. It is an area for exploration. Group sessions for Hypnotic Beatboxing could benefit several people at a time.

Lecturing

The forums for lecturing and teaching are vast. There will always be someone needed to present on topics. The same is true for Hypnotic Beatboxing and hypnosis. Raising awareness and equipping people to circulate and utilize Hypnotic Beatboxing techniques is a very useful field. There are many people being paid a good deal of money to teach new forms and new topics.

Recording Hypnotic Beatboxing

The recording musician is really no different from a recording Hypnotic Beatboxer. New music always needs to be recorded to be more circulated. While Hypnotic Beatboxing is not necessarily a musical genre per se, it is a recording form. People can get paid to do or sell their own recordings for hire in a freelance. With a little training and practice one could make themself available for a Hypnotic Beatboxing recording session this is able to be done in two forms. First, is the hypnotic suggestion being recorded. Many people are doing this already. The second less obvious way is to record the beatbox ambient tracks for hypnosis. One could either record both the hypnotic suggestion and the beatbox hypnotic formula or a single form of either of these.

Video Making of Hypnotic Beatboxing

Video making and its marketability is sort of a new thing. Not new as in brand new but new as in in the hands of many. Making hypnotic beatbox videos is almost a new genre. And in any genre of video making there is room for opportunity.

Training

Training is a little different than lecturing. Training is more in-depth and centralized. When one starts any form of training they take a class, classes, a whole module or career worth of training to work in a specific occupation. The same can be said of Hypnotic Beatboxing. Just as a hypnotist or hypnotherapist normally takes training. A Hypnotic Beatboxer could participate in formal training. Being the instructor of these classes could be a paid position.

Formula Writing

Some people might not want to write formulas but may be more interested in the beatboxing aspect of Hypnotic Beatboxing. And conversely so others may not want to beatbox but write formulas only. This a person gets paid to write.

Research

Research needs to be done to verify evidence basis for anything that is new. And the realms of Hypnosis and new therapies, research needs to be done. Being paid to research new topics and to fund ideas to enhance in play therapies such as hypnosis and Hypnotic Beatboxing are crucial in furthering the science and therapeutic value of treatments people recieve.

The Tasks of a Hypnotic Beatboxer

There are specific tasks a Hypnotic Beatboxer may have to perform on a regular basis. Some of these tasks can be periodically done and some are more frequent. They extend into various different infrastructures. This incorporates a professional decorum and inner workings with various different businesses and platforms. A list of tasks for a Hypnotic beatboxer is as follows:

- **Clinical practice**
- **Hospital visits**
- **Community outreach and awareness raising**
- **In-home treatment**
- **Therapies**
- **Paperwork and documentation**
- **Facilitating groups**
- **Teaching hypnotic beatboxing**
- **Recording hypnotic beatboxing audio**
- **Self-promotion or general marketing**
- **Humanitarian outreach**
- **Research**
- **Supervision of a team**

Clinical Practice

One-on-one Hypnotic Beatboxing therapy sessions can be a starting point for some clients. Some people perfer in-person encounters to video or auio. This can make it beneificial for a psychiatrist practice it if they so choose.

Hospital Visits

A hypnotist or a Hypnotic Beatboxer could make visits to a hospital to help people with pain or with mental health issues in their recoveries.

General community outreach and awareness raising

It is not out of the scope of Hypnotic Beatboxing to reach out to the community and make things better by spreading the knowledge of its applications through a broader awareness in the community. This can be done as an extension of clinical Hypnotic Beatboxing sessions.

In-Home Treatment

A Hypnotic Beatboxer could do an at-home session and there were boundaries of propriety and play this could be a very therapeutic endeavor for the client. At home is usually where people are most comfortable.

Therapies

While the scope of this book has been mostly on self-help there are numerous hypnosis-based therapies. Exploring them more within the Hypnotic Beatboxing format is something that has promise.

Paperwork and Documentation

Most mental health jobs and healthcare professions have documentation to do. This will probably be unavoidable for a Hypnotic Beatboxer. Such paperwork is necessary for much of billing as well as litigation purposes. It also ensures that people are getting the care they pay for and deserve.

Facilitating Groups

A Hypnotic Beatboxing group could be very therapeutic for multiple individuals at the same time. This enables more people to be served by using Hypnotic Beatboxing at a time then just one-on-one sessions. It can also reinforce private therapy or hypnotherapy as clients are also receiving the Hypnotic Beatbox therapy in the group.

Teaching Hypnotic Beatboxing

Colleges are a place for thought and growth. Hypnotic Beatboxing can benefit students in great ways. There could possibly be whole courses for Hypnotic Beatboxing. Plus a teacher can be paid.

Recording Hypnotic Beatboxing Audio

Recording Hypnotic Beatboxing is a fertile field for employment. Selling your recordings online may be the most reasonable format for this. Streaming your recordings is another viable solution to having people pay for your recordings.

Self-Promotion or General Marketing

Self-promotion of your Hypnotic Heatboxing product or service is necessary to spread the word about what you were doing.

Humanitarian Outreach

Leaving a legacy is important and helping the world be a better place is the right thing to do. A Hypnotic Beatboxer may be tied into a practice, but this does a person should not reach beyond the scope of their day today. As a Hypnotic Beatboxer one could influence the world for better in powerful ways.

Research

To keep yourself sharp and accurate you need to do your research. Techniques and problems change so keeping an edge on the workings and current facts and stastistics on research is crucial to keeping pertinent.

Supervision of A Team

Supervision implies a hierarchy of having a team. If you have worked hard enough and been successful, you could have a team of Hypnotic Beatboxers that reaches out to a certain community. This enhances the scope of your practice. It is a great responsibility but also a privilege to be enjoyed.

The Barriers of Hypnotic Beatboxing

With any emerging field that offers promise there are obstacles and barriers. These barriers span several different areas of being a hypnotic field that is largely unknown. There are always the technical difficulties of getting up and running and credibility. The road to a successful Hypnotic Beatboxing practice is fraught with barriers. The barriers of Hypnotic Beatboxing include:

- **Knowledge of the field**
- **Training**
- **Awareness**
- **Acceptance of the application**
- **Evidence Basis and research**
- **Certification**
- **Funding**
- **Legal**
- **Stigma**
- **Circulation**

Knowledge of the Field

Since Hypnotic Beatboxing is a new field there are not a whole lot of people that know about it. As more people become aware of Hypnotic Beatboxing the knowledge base of the field will expand. Research and learning will expand the knowledge base as well.

Training

There are not a lot of people equipped to train for Hypnotic Beatboxing careers. More people will be able to teach it as the field is more widely circulated.

Awareness

Awareness is along the same lines as the knowledge. Hypnotic Beatboxing is has to be Known as a technique of coping and a therapy to flourish.

Acceptance of the Application

Acceptance could be a very significant barrier to the circulation of Hypnotic Beatboxing. Hypnosis is not without controversy in the psychological field. Hypnotic Beatboxing could face some degree of scrutiny.

Evidence Basis and Research

There has been little specific research on Hypnotic Beatboxing. Finding evidence for or against it is necessary. My applications are based off of the standing research of hypnosis, positive thinking, and breathing exercises from their evidence basis. They are a strong proofs for the efficacy of Hypnotic Beatboxing.

Certification

Many programs including hypnosis have certifications that are necessary to work in the field. Being recognized in society as a viable and legitimate business is necessary. There is probably no exception for Hypnotic Beatboxing. With its circulation will come needs for certification.

Funding

Being a new field there is little available for Hypnotic Beatboxing. It can work within the systems already in-play but it would have to get funding to be more circulated. For people to be paid to practice it and for products to be made, funding would be needed.

Legal

Most every business has some legality issues surrounding it. The government has regulations on just about everything through laws and the justice system.

Stigma

Hypnosis has stigma attached to it. People think it is quackery and that it is on baseless claims or anecdotal evidence. There is room for acceptance of this field as Hypnotic Beatboxing is new and research and evidence is made known. Beatboxing alone has faced some rejection by certain people in the community. Statements such as "why don't you use real instruments" or "that is rap" show a lack of insight into what beatboxing is. When people do not know about or relate to something they often lable it or avoid it. This is likely to be true of Hypnotic Beatboxing because it is a blen of Hypnosis and Beatboxing both of which are stigmatized.

Circulation

The Circulation or spread of Hypnotic Beatboxing would be necessary to spread this form of hypnosis. Getting more people to see and use it is necessary for it to be understood and applied. Hypnotic Beatboxing is not at this place of wide circulation yet.

The church setting it is referred to by certain circles as a place of worship. The place you worship is often in a building. The acts of worship can be done with or without the building. It is a gathering so-to-speak. This kind of concept could be said of any community uses a building in order to function. Many businesses require buildings or at least some kind of physical structure to house their work. In today's world of Internet basis, it is quite possible to cut out some of the overhead. We will discuss using this to your advantage. Some of the technical details are as follows:

- **Your office**
- **Your schedule**
- **Your clients/patients**
- **Working within the different infrastructures**
- **Your team**
- **Overhead**
- **Investments**
- **Equipment**
- **Website**
- **Ebooks, paperback, audio and video**
- **Travel expenses**
- **Taxes**
- **Advertisements and marketing**

Your Office

Most every business needs some form of office to deal with the order of things. This office could be scheduling for meetings for planning and for general work. For a Hypnotic Beatboxer this may be a little different but you still need a place to work.

Your Schedule

Scheduling can be a little more involved than an office. Things includes who to meet with, how to work, and how to plan your day-to-day routine. A Hypnotic Beatboxer's schedule will vary depending on the individual's workload and obligations. Your schedule and time management is of utmost importance.

Your Clients, Patients, or Customers

Your clientele are the people that you take care of the people that you help or meet with to provide Hypnotic Beatboxing or products (audio, video or lessons). Your clients may be in person or through a telehealth. You may be able to meet with people far off or at your house or at their house or in a clinic setting. Patients and clients are what makes blood flow in a therapeutic session. You provide a specific service that helps a specific person

Working within the Different Infrastructures

There are already facilities for behavioral Health, mental health clinics, hypnosis clinics, rehabilitation centers and hospitals. Being able to carve into one of these niches could be crucial and being successful as a Hypnotic Beatboxer. To conserve your energy and time and resources try to work within the frameworks already available to you through current infrastructures available to you.

Your Team

For many people their team is just "me". If you are in this business by yourself you may not employ other people. If you have a good degree of success, you may want to have the help of others so you can reach more people and improve more lives. Having a team has benefits but it also has costs such as insurance, payroll taxes benefits etc. In today's world your team does not necessarily have to meet in "your" building. Teams can be largely internet-based from afar off. A partnership is when you are not the sole owner of the business but a share it with a member or team of members. This lightens up the load a little financially as well as structurally.

Overhead

Overhead can be expensive. This inludes but is not limited to rent, lights, electricity and various maintenance issues. If you're overhead is just at your house, then a lot of your overhead is shaved off. Overhead is something you always want to consider well trying to start a new business.

Investments

Investments take on many forms. Investments could be equipment for recording, new products to sell, or manufacturing materials to make products, in new research or new techniques for employees. Investment is a good way for a business to grow.

Equipment

Equipment for live play, recording or web based interactions is vital. You may want to invest in a decent computer system for live interactions with clients. When it comes to Hypnotic Beatboxing do not sell yourself short on investing in equipment. Quality equipment can save you a lot of headaches and long run.

Website

It has been said that a website is like a storefront. Having an up and running website for Hypnotic Beatboxing endeavors gives you credibility. It also gives you an outlet for people to look up your material or make purchases and sign up for services. A website is a must for a Hypnotic Beatboxer.

Ebooks, Paperback, Audio and Video

Ebooks, paperback, audio and video are all modes for dispersing Hypnotic Beatboxing materials. There are many companies to assist you in this. You can do a lot of this on your own. That choice is up to you but there are many price ranges to factor as well as some drawbacks and some benefits to each of these choices. Do your research to find out what may be the best packages or techniques for getting your products and services out there.

Travel Expenses

Traveling is a potential option for Hypnotic Beatboxer if they are going to present or teach. You can do this by merely meeting in a teleconference, but traveling may be unavoidable if you want to reach certain crowds. Always factor in your travel expenses.

Taxes, yes taxes

As with any business a Hypnotic Beatboxer will have to pay his taxes. If you earn a paycheck make sure you file properly so you do not face trouble in the long run. Pay your employees taxes and your taxes. Be aware of tax changes and also potential benefits you may be able to have as a business owner.

HYPNOTIC BEATBOXING FORMULA PATTERNS

Relaxation-Bass Kick (Formula Pattern)

Breathe in for four seconds.

 bb I am calm **bb**

bb and relaxed. I go deeper **bb** and deeper into relaxation.

bb I am peaceful, loose, limp, **bb** and relaxed.

bb I go deeper and deeper into relaxation **bb** I am comfortable.

bb I am peaceful **bb** and relaxed.

bb I let go of my thoughts and feelings **bb** and embrace peace and relaxation

Repeat.

Relaxation-Snare (Formula Pattern)

Breathe in for four seconds.

kk I am calm **kk**

kk and relaxed. I go deeper **kk** and deeper into relaxation.

kk I am peaceful, loose, limp, **kk** and relaxed.

kk I go deeper and deeper into relaxation **kk** I am comfortable

kk I am peaceful **kk** and relaxed.

kk I let go of my thoughts and feelings **kk** and embrace peace and relaxation **kk**.

Repeat.

Relaxation-Heartbeat Breath (Formula Pattern)

Breathe in for four seconds.

 ug ug I (*inhale* **i**) am calm **ug ug** (*exhale* **e**)

ug ug and relaxed. (*inhale* **i**) I go deeper **ug ug** and deeper into relaxation (*exhale* **e**).

ug ug I am peaceful, (*inhale* **i**) loose, limp, **ug ug** and relaxed (*exhale* **e**).

ug ug I go deeper and deeper into (*inhale* **i**) relaxation **ug ug** I am comfortable (*exhale* **e**).

ug ug I (*inhale* **i**) am peaceful **ug ug** and relaxed   (*exhale* **e**).

ug ug I let go of my thoughts and feelings (*inhale* **i**) **ug ug** and embrace peace and relaxation.

Repeat.

Relaxation-Full Drum (Formula Pattern)

Breathe in for four seconds.

 btkt I am calm **btkt**

btkt and relaxed. I go deeper **btkt** and deeper into relaxation.

btkt I am peaceful, loose, limp, **btkt** and relaxed.

btkt I go deeper and deeper into relaxation **btkt** I am comfortable

btkt I am peaceful **btkt** and relaxed.

btkt I let go of my thoughts and feelings **btkt** and embrace peace and relaxation **btkt**.

Repeat.

Quitting Smoking-Bass Kick (Formula Pattern)

Breathe in for four seconds.

bb I have enough **bb.**

bb I am **bb** complete.

bb I can live **bb**

bb a life without smoking **bb**.

bb I enjoy **bb**

bb the benefits of a healthy **bb** lifestyle.

Repeat.

Quitting Smoking-Snare (Formula Pattern)

Breathe in for four seconds.

kk I have enough **kk.**

kk I am **kk** complete.

kk I can live **kk**

kk a life without smoking **kk.**

kk I enjoy **kk**

kk the benefits of a healthy **kk** lifestyle.

Repeat.

Quitting Smoking-Heartbeat Breath

(Formula Pattern)

Breathe in for four seconds.

ug ug I (*inhale* **i**) have enough **ug ug** (*exhale* **e**).

ug ug I (*inhale* **i**) am **ug ug** complete(*exhale* **e**).

ug ug I (*inhale* **i**) can live **ug ug** (*exhale* **e**)

ug ug a life (*inhale* **i**) without smoking **ug ug** (*exhale* **e**).

ug ug I (*inhale* **i**) enjoy **ug ug** (*exhale* **e**)

ug ug the benefits (*inhale* **i**) of a healthy **ug ug** lifestyle (*exhale* **e**).

Repeat.

Quitting Smoking-Full Drum (Formula Pattern)

Breathe in for four seconds.

b t k I have enough **t t k.**

b t k I am **t t k** complete.

b t k I can live **t t k**

b t k a life without smoking **t t k.**

b t k I enjoy **t t k.**

b t k the benefits of a healthy **t t k** lifestyle.

Repeat.

Harm Reduction-Bass Kick (Formula Pattern)

Breathe in for four seconds.

bb I have enough **bb.**

bb I am **bb** complete.

bb I can choose **bb**

bb to say no or to say yes, **bb** to substances.

bb I can reduce my using easily **bb.**

bb I enjoy my ability to say yes or no **bb** and to cut back

bb and be healthier.

Repeat.

Harm Reduction-Snare (Formula Pattern)

Breathe in for four seconds.

kk I have enough **kk.**

kk I am **kk** complete.

kk I can choose **kk**

kk to say no or to say yes, **kk** to substances.

kk I can reduce my using easily **kk.**

kk I enjoy my ability to say yes or no **kk** and to cut back **kk** and be healthier.

Repeat.

Harm Reduction-Heartbeat Breath

(Formula Pattern)

Breathe in for four seconds.

ug ug I (*inhale* **i)** have enough **ug ug** (*exhale* **e).**

ug ug I (*inhale* **i)** am **ug ug** complete (*exhale* **e).**

ug ug I (*inhale* **i)** can choose **ug ug** (*exhale* **e)**

ug ug to say no (*inhale* **i)** or to say yes, **ug ug** to substances (*exhale* **e).**

ug ug I (*inhale* **i)** can reduce my using easily **ug ug** (*exhale* **e).**

ug ug I enjoy (*inhale* **i)** my ability to say yes or no **ug ug** and to cut back **ug ug** and be healthier (*exhale* **e).**

Repeat.

Harm Reduction-Full Drum (Formula Pattern)

Breathe in for four seconds.

btkt I have enough **btkt.**

btkt I am **btkt** complete.

btkt I can choose **btkt**

btkt to say no or to say yes, **btkt** to substances.

btkt I can reduce my using easily **btkt.**

btkt I enjoy my ability to say yes or no **btkt** and to cut back **btkt** and be healthier.

Repeat.

Coping with Anxiety-Bass Kick

(Formula Pattern)

Breathe in for four seconds.

bb I am calm **bb.**

bb I am **bb** confident.

bb I can handle **bb** any fear**.**

bb I am strong I am good **bb** I am comfortable.

bb I am peaceful **bb.**

bb I can handle all things **bb.**

Repeat.

Coping with Anxiety-Snare (Formula Pattern)

Breathe in for four seconds.

kk I am calm **kk.**

kk I am **kk** confident.

kk I can handle **kk** any fear**.**

kk I am strong. I am good **kk** I am comfortable.

kk I am peaceful **kk.**

kk I canhandle all things **kk**

Repeat.

Coping with Anxiety-Heartbeat Breath

(Formula Pattern)

Breathe in for four seconds.

ug ug I (*inhale* **i**) am calm **ug ug** (*exhale* **e**).

ug ug I (*inhale* **i**) am **ug ug** confident (*exhale* **e**).

ug ug I (*inhale* **i**) can handle **ug ug** any fear (*exhale* **e**).

ug ug I am strong (*inhale* **i**) I am good **ug ug**   I am comfortable (*exhale* **e**).

ug ug I (*inhale* **i**) am peaceful **ug ug** (*exhale* **e**).

ug ug   I can (*inhale* **i**) handle all things **ug ug** in life (*exhale* **e**).

Repeat.

Coping with Anxiety-Full Drum

(Formula Pattern)

Breathe in for four seconds.

b t k I am calm **t t k**.

btkt I am **t t k** confident.

b t k I can handle **t t k** any fear.

b t k I am strong I am good **t t k** I am comfortable.

b t k I am peacefu **t t k**.

b t k I can (*inhale* **i**) handle all things **t t k**.

Repeat.

Coping with Stress-Bass Kick (Formula Pattern)

Breathe in for four seconds.

bb I am calm **bb** and relaxed.

bb I can handle any stresses and challenges **bb** in lfe.

bb I am complete **bb** and strong.

bb nothing is to difficult to overcome **bb**.

bb I can be calm **bb** and relaxed.

bb even when life is difficult **bb**.

Repeat.

Coping with Stress-Snare (Formula Pattern)

Breathe in for four seconds.

kk I am calm **kk** and relaxed.

kk I can handle any stresses and challenges **kk** in lfe.

kk I am complete **kk** and strong.

kk nothing is to difficult to overcome **kk**.

kk I can be calm **kk** and relaxed.

kk even when life is difficult **kk**.

Repeat.

Coping with Stress-Heartbeat Breath

(Formula Pattern)

Breathe in for four seconds.

ug ug I (*inhale* **i**) am calm **ug ug** and relaxed (*exhale* **e**).

ug ug I can handle any (*inhale* **i**) stresses and challenges **ug ug** in lfe(*exhale* **e**).

ug ug I am (*inhale* **i**) complete **ug ug** and strong (*exhale* **e**).

ug ug nothing (*inhale* **i**) is to difficult to overcome **ug ug** (*exhale* **e**).

ug ug I (*inhale* **i**) can be calm **ug ug** and relaxed(*exhale* **e**).

ug ug even when (*inhale* **i**) life is difficult **ug ug** (*exhale* **e**).

Repeat.

Coping with Stress-Full Drum (Formula Pattern)

Breathe in for four seconds.

b t k I am calm **t t k** and relaxed.

b t k I can handle any stresses and challenges **t t k** in lfe.

b t k I am complete **t t k** and strong.

b t k nothing is to difficult to overcome **t t k**.

b t k I can be calm **t t k** and relaxed.

b t k even when life is difficult **t t k**.

Repeat.

Coping with Depression-Bass Kick

(Formula Pattern)

Breathe in for four seconds.

bb I am happy **bb.**

bb I am **bb** more than enough.

bb I am positive **bb** and complete.

bb I feel good and see hope **bb**

bb in each day. There is always potential for **bb** good in life.

bb I am happy and content **bb** in life.

Repeat.

Coping with Depression-Snare

(Formula Pattern)

Breathe in for four seconds.

kk I am happy **kk.**

kk I am **kk** more than enough.

kk I am positive **kk** and complete.

kk I feel good and see hope **kk**

kk in each day. There is always potential for **kk** good in life.

kk I am happy and content **kk** in life.

Repeat.

Coping with Depression-Heartbeat Breath

(Formula Pattern)

Breathe in for four seconds.

ug ug I (*inhale* **i**) am happy **ug ug** (*exhale* **e**).

ug ug I (*inhale* **i**) am **ug ug** more than enough (*exhale* **e**).

ug ug I (*inhale* **i**) am positive **ug ug** and complete(*exhale* **e**).

ug ug feel good (*inhale* **i**) and see hope **ug ug** (*exhale* **e**)

ug ug in each day. **(***inhale* **i)** There is always potential for **ug ug** good in life(*exhale* **e**).

ug ug I (*inhale* **i**) am happy and content **ug ug** in life (*exhale* **e**).

Repeat.

Coping with Depression Full Drum

(Formula Pattern)

Breathe in for four seconds.

b t k I am happy **t t k.**

b t k I am **t t k** more than enough.

b t k I am positive **t t k** and complete.

b t k I feel good and see hope **t t k**

b t k in each day. There is always potential for **t t k** good in life.

b t k I am happy and content **t t k** in life.

Repeat.

Coping with Anger-Bass Kick

(Formula Pattern)

Breathe in for four seconds.

bb I am calm **bb**

bb and relaxed. **bb** I am relaxing **bb** deeper and deeper.

bb I am in control of my feelings and thoughts. **bb** I have respect and dignity.

bb I can handle confrontation effectively **bb** and things will not bother me as much.

bb in each day I see the good in me and the world around me **bb** and be calm.

bb I am happy and content **bb** I am calm.

Repeat.

Coping with Anger-Snare

(Formula Pattern)

Breathe in for four seconds.

kk I am calm **kk**

kk and relaxed. **kk** I am relaxing **kk** deeper and deeper.

kk I am in control of my feelings and thoughts. **kk** I have respect and dignity.

kk I can handle confrontation effectively **kk** and things will not bother me as much.

kk in each day I see the good in me and the world around me **kk** and be calm.

kk I am happy and content **kk** I am calm.

Repeat.

Coping with Anger-Heartbeat Breath (Formula Pattern)

Breathe in for four seconds.

ug ug I (*inhale* **i**) am calm **ug ug** (*exhale* **e**)

ug ug and relaxed. (*inhale* **i**) I am relaxing **ug ug** deeper and deeper (*exhale* **e**).

ug ug I (*inhale* **i**) am in control of my feelings and thoughts. **ug ug** I have respect and dignity(*exhale* **e**).

ug ug I can (*inhale* **i**) handle confrontation effectively

ug ug and things will not bother me as much(*exhale* **e**).

ug ug in each day (*inhale* **i**) I see the good in me and the

world around me **ug ug** and be calm (*exhale* **e**).

ug ug I (*inhale* **i**) am happy and content **ug ug** I am calm

(*exhale* **e**).

Repeat.

Coping with Anger-Full Drum (Formula Pattern)

Breathe in for four seconds.

b t k t I am calm **t t k**

b t k t and relaxed. I am relaxing **kk** deeper and deeper.

b t k t I am in control of my feelings and thoughts **t t k** I have respect and dignity.

b t k t I can handle confrontation effectively **t t k** and things will not bother me as much.

b t k t in each day I see the good in me and the world around me **t t k** and be calm.

b t k t I am happy and content **t t k** I am calm.

Repeat.

Eating Healthy-Bass Kick (Formula Pattern)

Breathe in for four seconds.

bb I can eat **bb**

bb healthy choices and portions **bb** of food.

bb I enjoy healthy foods **bb.**

bb Healthy eating is a lifestyle I thoroughly **bb** enjoy.

bb I enjoy **bb**

bb the benefits of a healthy **bb** lifestyle.

Repeat.

Eating Healthy Snare (Formula Pattern)

Breathe in for four seconds.

kk I can eat **kk**

kk healthy choices and portions **kk** of food.

kk I enjoy healthy foods **kk.**

kk Healthy eating is a lifestyle I thoroughly **kk** enjoy.

kk I enjoy **kk**

kk the benefits of a healthy **kk** lifestyle.

Repeat.

Eating Healthy-Heartbeat Breath

(Formula Pattern)

Breathe in for four seconds.

ug ug I (*inhale* **i**) can eat **ug ug** (*exhale* **e**)

ug ug healthy choices (*inhale* **i**) and portions **ug ug** of food (*exhale* **e**).

ug ug I (*inhale* **i**) enjoy healthy foods **ug ug** (*exhale* **e**).

ug ug Healthy eating (*inhale* **i**) is a lifestyle I thoroughly **ug ug** enjoy(*exhale* **e**).

ug ug I (*inhale* **i**) enjoy **ug ug** (*exhale* **e**)

ug ug the benefits (*inhale* **i**) of a healthy **ug ug** lifestyle (*exhale* **e**).

Repeat.

Eating Healthy-Full Drum (Formula Pattern)

Breathe in for four seconds.

b t k t I can eat **t t k**

b t k t healthy choices and portions **t t k** of food.

b t k t I enjoy healthy foods **t t k.**

b t k t Healthy eating is a lifestyle I thoroughly **t t k**
enjoy.

b t k t I (*inhale* **i**) enjoy **t t k**

b t k t the benefits of a healthy **t t k** lifestyle.

Repeat.

Increasing Exercise-Bass Kick

(Formula Pattern)

Breathe in for four seconds.

bb I can be healthy **bb.**

bb exercise can be fun **bb** and I am motivated.

bb Exercise is enjoyable enjoy the benefits **bb** of exercise.

bb Exercising is easy **bb.**

bb I enjoy **bb**

bb the benefits of a healthy **bb** lifestyle.

Repeat.

Increasing Exercise-Snare (Formula Pattern)

Breathe in for four seconds.

kk I can be healthy **kk.**

kk exercise can be fun **kk** and I am motivated.

kk Exercise is enjoyable enjoy the benefits **kk** of exercise.

kk Exercising is easy **kk.**

kk I enjoy **kk**

kk the benefits of a healthy **kk** lifestyle.

Repeat.

Increasing Exercise Heartbeat Breath

(Formula Pattern)

Breathe in for four seconds.

ug ug I (*inhale* **i)** can be healthy **ug ug** (*exhale* **e).**

ug ug Exercise can (*inhale* **i)** be fun **ug ug** and I am motivated (*exhale* **e).**

ug ug I (*inhale* **i)** enjoy the benefits **ug ug** of exercise(*exhale* **e).**

ug ug exercise is (*inhale* **i)** is easy **ug ug** (*exhale* **e).**

ug ug I (*inhale* **i)** enjoy **ug ug** (*exhale* **e)**

ug ug the benefits (*inhale* **i)** of a healthy **ug ug** lifestyle (*exhale* **e).**

Repeat.

Increasing Exercise-Full Drum

(Formula Pattern)

Breathe in for four seconds.

b t k t I can be healthy **t t k.**

b t k t exercise can be fun **t t k** and I am motivated.

b t k t Exercise is enjoyable enjoy the benefits **bb** of exercise.

b t k t Exercising is easy **t t k**.

b t k t I enjoy **t t k**

b t k t the benefits of a healthy **t t k** lifestyle.

Repeat.

Increasing Motivation-Bass Kick

(Formula Pattern)

Breathe in for four seconds.

bb I have strength **bb.**

bb I have energy and drive **bb** to get things done.

bb I can follow through with things **bb**

bb and accomplish anything I set out to do **bb.**

bb I enjoy **bb**

bb the accomplishments of my **bb** hard work.

Repeat.

Increasing Motivation-Snare (Formula Pattern)

Breathe in for four seconds.

kk I have strength **kk.**

kk I have energy and drive **kk** to get things done.

kk I can follow through with things **kk**

kk and accomplish anything I set out to do **kk.**

kk I enjoy **kk**

kk the accomplishments of my **kk** hard work.

Repeat.

Increasing Motivation-Heartbeat Breath

(Formula Pattern)

Breathe in for four seconds.

ug ug I (*inhale* **i**) have strength **ug ug** (*exhale* **e**).

ug ug I have energy (*inhale* **i**) and drive **ug ug** to get things done (*exhale* **e**).

ug ug I (*inhale* **i**) can follow through with things **ug ug** (*exhale* **e**).

ug ug and accomplish (*inhale* **i**) anything I set out to do **ug ug** (*exhale* **e**).

ug ug I (*inhale* **i**) enjoy **ug ug** (*exhale* **e**).

ug ug the accomplishments (*inhale* **i**) of my **ug ug** hard work (*exhale* **e**).

Repeat.

Increasing Motivation-Full Drum

(Formula Pattern)

Breathe in for four seconds.

b t k t I have strength **t t k.**

b t k t I have energy and drive **t t k** to get things done.

b t k t I can follow through with things **t t k.**

b t k t and accomplish anything I set out to do **t t k**.

b t k t I enjoy **t t k**

b t k t the accomplishments of my **t t k** hard work.

Repeat.

Reaching Goals-Bass Kick

(Formula Pattern)

Breathe in for four seconds.

bb I am calm **bb.**

bb I am relaxed and focused **bb** and intent on getting things done.

bb I can prioritize effectively **bb** and zero in on any task**.**

bb I can be timely **bb** and accomplish all necessary tasks.

bb I can set goals I can reach goals **bb** and reach them**.**

bb I am able to get things done, **bb** No task is too

difficult. I can also share responsibilities with other people.

Repeat.

Reaching Goals-Snare (Formula Pattern)

Breathe in for four seconds.

kk I am calm **kk.**

kk I am relaxed and focused **kk** and intent on getting things done.

kk I can prioritize effectively **kk** and zero in on any task.

kk I can be timely **kk** and accomplish all necessary tasks.

kk I can set goals I can reach goals **kk** and reach them.

kk I am able to get things done, **kk** No task is too difficult. I can also share responsibilities with other people.

Repeat.

Reaching Goals-Heartbeat Breath

(Formula Pattern)

Breathe in for four seconds.

ug ug I (*inhale* **i)** am calm **ug ug** (*exhale* **e)**

ug ug and relaxed. (*inhale* **i)** I am focused **ug ug** and
intent on getting things done (*exhale* **e)**.

ug ug I (*inhale* **i)** can prioritize effectively **ug ug** and zero in

on any task (*exhale* **e).**

ug ug I can (*inhale* **i)** be timely **ug ug** and accomplish all

necessary tasks (*exhale* **e)**.

ug ug I can set goals (*inhale* **i) and** reach them **ug ug**

(*exhale* **e).**

ug ug I (*inhale* **i)** am able to get things done. **ug ug** No

task is too difficult (*exhale* **e)**. I can also share

responsibilities with other people.

Repeat.

Reaching Goals-Full Drum (Formula Pattern)

Breathe in for four seconds. Hold for seven seconds. Breathe out a beat for eight seconds.

Breathe in for four seconds.

b t k t I am calm **bb.**

b t k t I am relaxed and focused **t t k** and intent on getting things done.

b t k t I can prioritize effectively **t t k** and zero in on any task.

b t k t I can be timely **t t k** and accomplish all necessary tasks.

b t k t I can set goals I can reach goals **t t k** and reach them.

b t k t I am able to get things done, **t t k** No task is too difficult. I can also share responsibilities with other people.

Repeat.

Fill in the Blank-Bass Kick (Formula Pattern)

Breathe in for four seconds.

bb I am ______________**bb.**

bb As I relax, I go deeper **bb** and deeper.

bb I am ____________ loose, limp, **bb** and relaxed.

bb I ____________ and____________ **bb** I can

____________ .

bb I am able to ____________**bb.**

bb I can____________ **bb** and ____________

Repeat.

Fill in the Blank-Snare (Formula Pattern)

Breathe in for four seconds.

kk I am ____________**kk.**

kk As I relax, I go deeper **kk** and deeper.

kk I am ____________ loose, limp, **kk** and relaxed.

kk I ____________ and____________ **kk** I can

____________ .

kk I am able to ____________**kk.**

kk I can____________ **kk** and ____________

Repeat.

Fill in the Blank-Heartbeat Breath (Formula Pattern)

Breathe in for four seconds.

ug ug I (*inhale* **i**) am ______________ **ug ug** (*exhale* **e**).

ug ug I relax (*inhale* **i**) I go deeper **ug ug** and deeper (*exhale* **e**).

ug ug I am ______________ (*inhale* **i**) loose, limp, **ug ug** and relaxed (*exhale* **e**).

ug ug I ______________ (*inhale* **i**) and______________ **ug ug** I can ______________ (*exhale* **e**).

ug ug I (*inhale* **i**) am able to ______________ **ug ug** (*exhale* **e**).

ug ug I can______________ (*inhale* **i**) **ug ug** and

______________.

Repeat.

Fill in the-Full Drum (Formula Pattern)

Breathe in for four seconds.

b t k t I am ___________ **t t k.**

b t k t As I relax, I go deeper **t t k** and deeper.

b t k t I am ___________ loose, limp, **t t k** and relaxed.

b t k t I ___________ and ___________ **t t k** I can

___________ .

b t k t I am able to ___________ **t t k.**

b t k t I can ___________ **t t k** and ___________

Repeat.

HYPNOTIC BEATBOXING TEMPLATES

Formula Template-Basekick

bb________bb________bb________bb________bb__________

bb________bb________bb________bb________bb__________

bb________bb________bb________bb________bb__________

bb________bb________bb________bb________bb__________

bb________bb________bb________bb________bb__________

bb________bb________bb________bb________bb__________

bb________bb________bb________bb________bb__________

bb________bb________bb________bb________bb__________

Formula Template-Snare

kk______kk______ kk_______ kk_______ kk__________

kk_______kk_______ kk_______ kk_______ kk__________

kk_______kk_______ kk_______ kk_______ kk__________

kk_______kk_______ kk_______ kk_______ kk__________

kk_______kk_______ kk_______ kk_______ kk__________

kk_______kk_______ kk_______ kk_______ kk__________

kk_______kk_______ kk_______ kk_______ kk__________

kk_______kk_______ kk_______ kk_______ kk__________

Formula Template-Shaker

shsh_______ shsh _______ shsh ________ shsh___________

shsh_______ shsh _______ shsh ________ shsh___________

shsh_______ shsh _______ shsh ________ shsh___________

shsh_______ shsh _______ shsh ________ shsh___________

Formula Template Heartbeat

ug ug__________ ug ug _______ ug ug __________ ug ug _______

ug ug__________ ug ug _______ ug ug __________ ug ug _______

ug ug__________ ug ug _______ ug ug __________ ug ug _______

ug ug__________ ug ug _______ Ug ug __________ ug ug _______

ug ug__________ ug ug _______ ug ug __________ ug ug _______

ug ug__________ ug ug _______ ug ug __________ ug ug _______

ug ug__________ ug ug _______ ug ug __________ ug ug _______

ug ug__________ ug ug _______ ug ug __________ ug ug _______

Formula Template-Bass Kick

bb________bb__________bb______________bb________bb________

bb________bb____________bb________bb____________bb________

bb________bb________bb______________bb________bb________

bb________bb____________bb________bb____________bb________

bb________bb__________bb______________bb________bb________

bb________bb______________bb________bb____________bb________

Formula Template-Hi-hat

tt__________ tt________________ tt ___________ tt __________

tt__________ tt________________ tt ___________ tt __________

tt__________ tt________________ tt ___________ tt __________

tt__________ tt________________ tt ___________ tt __________

tt__________ tt________________ tt ___________ tt __________

tt__________ tt________________ tt ___________ tt __________

Formula Template-Hi-hat

tt_______ tt________ tt ______ tt _______ tt _______ tt______

tt______ tt________ tt ______ tt _______ tt _______ tt______

tt_______ tt________ tt ______ tt _______ tt _______ tt______

tt______ tt________ tt ______ tt _______ tt _______ tt______

tt______ tt________ tt ______ tt _______ tt _______ tt______

tt______ tt________ tt ______ tt _______ tt _______ tt______

tt______ tt________ tt ______ tt _______ tt _______ tt______

tt_______ tt________ tt ______ tt _______ tt _______ tt______

Formula Template-Shaker

sh sh_____________ sh sh __________ sh sh_______________

sh sh_____________ sh sh __________ sh sh_______________

sh sh_____________ sh sh __________ sh sh_______________

sh sh_____________ sh sh __________ sh sh_______________

sh sh_____________ sh sh __________ sh sh_______________

sh sh_____________ sh sh __________ sh sh_______________

Formula Template-Shaker, Snare and Hi-hat

sh t k t______ t k t _______sh t k t _______ tt k t _________

sh t k t______ t k t _______sh t k t _______ tt k t _________

sh t k t______ t k t _______sh t k t _______ tt k t _________

sh t k t______ t k t _______sh t k t _______ tt k t _________

sh t k t______ t k t _______sh t k t _______ tt k t _________

sh t k t______ t k t _______sh t k t _______ tt k t _________

Formula Template-Bass Kick, Snare and Hi-hat

b t t________ t k t___ b t t t______ t k t__________

b t t________ t k t___ b t t t______ t k t__________

b t t________ t k t___ b t t t______ t k t__________

b t t________ t k t___ b t t t______ t k t__________

b t t________ t k t___ b t t t______ t k t__________

b t t________ t k t___ b t t t______ t k t__________

Formula Template-Bass Kick, Snare and Hi-hat

b t t________ t k t___ b t t t______ t k t__________

b t t t______ t k t__________________ b t t t

______t k t____ b t t t ______t k t___ b t t t

______t k t____ b t t t ______t k t____ b t t t

____t k t____ b t t t ____t k t___ b t t t

____t k t____ b t t t ______t k t____ b t t t

____t k t___ b t t t ______t k t____ b t t t

__t k t___ b t t t

Formula-Template Snare

kk _________ kk _________ kk _________ kk_________

kk _________ kk _________ kk _________ kk_________

kk _________ kk _________ kk _________ kk_________

kk _________ kk _________ kk _________ kk_________

kk _________ kk _________ kk _________ kk_________

kk _________ kk _________ kk _________ kk_________

Formula Template-Snare and Hi-hat

t t k t _____ t t k t _____ t t k t ___ t t k t __________

t t k t _____ t t k t _____ t t k t ___ t t k t _________

t t k t _____ t t k t _____ t t k t ___ t t k t _________

t t k t _____ t t k t _____ t t k t ___ t t k t ________

t t k t _____ t t k t _____ t t k t ___ t t k t ________

t t k t _____ t t k t _____ t t k t ___ t t k t ________

t t k t _____ t t k t _____ t t k t ___ t t k t ________

t t k t _____ t t k t _____ t t k t ___ t t k t ________

Formula Template-Snare and Hi-hat

k t k t ___ k t k t ____ k t k t ___ k t k t ______

k t k t ___ k t k t ___ k t k t ___ k t k t ______

k t k t ___ k t k t ___ k t k t ___ k t k t ______

k t k t ___ k t k t ___ k t k t ___ k t k t ______

k t k t ___ k t k t ____ k t k t ___ k t k t ______

k t k t ___ k t k t ____ k t k t ___ k t k t ______

k t k t ___ k t k t ___ k t k t ___ k t k t ______

k t k t ___ k t k t ___ k t k t ___ k t k t ______

Formula Template-Heartbeat Breath

ug ug_____i_______ ug ug _________e_______

ug ug_____i_______ ug ug _________e_______

 ug ug_____i_______ ug ug _________e_______

ug ug_____i_______ ug ug _________e_______

ug ug_____i_______ ug ug _________e_______

ug ug_____i_______ ug ug _________e_______

Formula Template-Inhale and Exhale

i__________e__________ i__________e__________

i__________e__________ i__________e__________

i__________e__________ i__________e__________

i__________e__________ i__________e__________

i__________e__________ i__________e__________

i__________e__________ i__________e__________

i__________e__________ i__________e__________

Formula Template-Snare and Hi-hat

kt_________ kt _________ kt _________ kt __________

kt_________ kt _________ kt _________ kt __________

kt_________ kt _________ kt _________ kt __________

kt_________ kt _________ kt _________ kt __________

kt_________ kt _________ kt _________ kt __________

kt_________ kt _________ kt _________ kt __________

WORKSHEETS AND TEMPLATES

Worksheets and Checklists

It can be very helpful to keep track of our progress. Worksheets are an effective way to do this. They provide us with a template of guidance and fill in the blank to help us be more specific with our progress. They help us gauge where we were, where we are, and where we might be or want to be as we try to change something in our life. The following pages give fill in the blanks and guiding questions other ways to track how you are doing.

Fill In the Blank Worksheet

Date: _______ Time:________

Things I want to change:___________________________

My mood before I do the Hypnotic Beatboxing formula or pattern:______________________________

The pattern I chose is:___________________________________

How many times I did a short phrase pattern:

____

How I felt after I did the pattern or formula:_______________________________

Formula or pattern I would like to try next:____________

Notes:____

____

____

____

____

____

____

Fill In the Blank Worksheet

Date: _________ Time:_________

Things I want to change:______________________

My mood before I do the Hypnotic Beatboxing formula or pattern:______________________

The pattern I chose is:______________________________

How many times I did a short phrase pattern:

____

How I felt after I did the pattern or formula:______________________

Formula or pattern I would like to try next:____________

Notes:______________________________________

____

____

____

____

____

____

Fill In the Blank Worksheet

Date: _______ Time:________

Things I want to change:___________________________

My mood before I do the Hypnotic Beatboxing formula or pattern:______________________________

The pattern I chose is:_________________________________

How many times I did a short phrase pattern:

____

How I felt after I did the pattern or formula:______________________________

Formula or pattern I would like to try next:______________

Notes:____

____

____

____

____

____

____

Fill In the Blank Worksheet

Date: _________ Time:_________

Things I want to change:_____________________

My mood before I do the Hypnotic Beatboxing formula or pattern:_____________________

The pattern I chose is:_____________________

How many times I did a short phrase pattern:

____

How I felt after I did the pattern or formula:_____________________

Formula or pattern I would like to try next:_____________

Notes:_____________________

____

____

____

____

____

____

Fill In the Blank Worksheet

Date: _______ Time:________

Things I want to change:_______________________

My mood before I do the Hypnotic Beatboxing formula or pattern:_____________________

The pattern I chose is:_________________________

How many times I did a short phrase pattern:

____

How I felt after I did the pattern or formula:__________________

Formula or pattern I would like to try next:___________

Notes:_______________________________

____

____

____

____

____

____

Fill In the Blank Worksheet

Date: _______ Time:________

Things I want to change:_____________________________

My mood before I do the Hypnotic Beatboxing formula or pattern:_____________________________

The pattern I chose is:_____________________________

How many times I did a short phrase pattern:

____

How I felt after I did the pattern or formula:_____________________________

Formula or pattern I would like to try next:____________

Notes:____

____

____

____

____

____

____

Fill In the Blank Worksheet

 Date: _______ Time:________

Things I want to change:______________________

My mood before I do the Hypnotic Beatboxing formula or pattern:_______________________

The pattern I chose is:____________________________

How many times I did a short phrase pattern:

____

How I felt after I did the pattern or formula:______________________

Formula or pattern I would like to try next:_____________

Notes:____

____

____

____

____

____

____

Fill In the Blank Worksheet

Date: _________ Time:_________

Things I want to change:_______________________

My mood before I do the Hypnotic Beatboxing formula or pattern:_______________________

The pattern I chose is:_______________________

How many times I did a short phrase pattern:

____

How I felt after I did the pattern or formula:_______________________

Formula or pattern I would like to try next:_____________

Notes:_______________________________

____

____

____

____

____

____

Fill In the Blank Worksheet

 Date: _______ Time:________

Things I want to change:___________________________

My mood before I do the Hypnotic Beatboxing formula or pattern:___________________________

The pattern I chose is:___________________________________

How many times I did a short phrase pattern:

____

How I felt after I did the pattern or formula:___________________________

Formula or pattern I would like to try next:_____________

Notes:____

____

____

____

____

____

____

Fill In the Blank Worksheet

 Date: _______ Time:_________

Things I want to change:_____________________________

My mood before I do the Hypnotic Beatboxing formula or pattern:_______________________________

The pattern I chose is:_________________________________

How many times I did a short phrase pattern:

____

How I felt after I did the pattern or formula:_______________________________

Formula or pattern I would like to try next:____________

Notes:____

____

____

____

____

____

____

Fill In the Blank Worksheet

Date: _______ Time:_________

Things I want to change:______________________________

My mood before I do the Hypnotic Beatboxing formula or pattern:______________________________

The pattern I chose is:______________________________

How many times I did a short phrase pattern:

____

How I felt after I did the pattern or formula:______________________

Formula or pattern I would like to try next:____________

Notes:______________________________________

____

____

____

____

____

____

Fill In the Blank Worksheet

Date: _________   Time:_________

Things I want to change:_______________________

My mood before I do the Hypnotic Beatboxing formula or pattern:_______________________

The pattern I chose is:___________________________

How many times I did a short phrase pattern:

____

How I felt after I did the pattern or formula:_______________________

Formula or pattern I would like to try next:___________

Notes:_____________________________________

____

____

____

____

____

____

Fill In the Blank Worksheet

Date:_______ Time:_______

Things I want to change.________________________

My mood before I do the hypnoboxics formula or pattern.________________________

The hypnoboxics pattern I chose is.________________________

How many times I did a hypnoboxics short phrase pattern.

____

How I felt after I did the hypnoboxics pattern or formula.___________________

Hypnoboxics formula or pattern I would like to try next._S
Notes:____________________________________

____

____

____

____

____

____

Fill In the Blank Worksheet

Date: _________ Time:_________

Things I want to change:_______________________________

My mood before I do the Hypnotic Beatboxing formula or pattern:_______________________________

The pattern I chose is:_______________________________

How many times I did a short phrase pattern:

____

How I felt after I did the pattern or formula:_______________________________

Formula or pattern I would like to try next:_____________

Notes:_______________________________

____

____

____

____

____

____

Fill In the Blank Worksheet

(Anxiety or Depression)

Date:_______Time:_________

Anxiety level 1 through 10. One is the least amount of anxiety 10 is the most circle one.

1 2 3 4 5 6 7 8 9 10

Hypnotic Beatboxing formula or pattern I chose:_____________

How do you feel after doing the pattern or formula:____

____

Formula or pattern you want to try next:_______________________

Notes:____

____

____

____

____

____

____

Fill In the Blank Worksheet

(Anxiety or Depression)

Date:_______Time:__________

Anxiety level 1 through 10. One is the least amount of anxiety 10 is the most circle one.

1 2 3 4 5 6 7 8 9 10

Hypnotic Beatboxing formula or pattern I chose:_____________

How do you feel after doing the pattern or formula:____

____

Formula or pattern you want to try next:______________________________

Notes:____

____

____

____

____

____

____

Fill In the Blank Worksheet

(Anxiety or Depression)

Date:________Time:__________

Anxiety level 1 through 10. One is the least amount of anxiety 10 is the most circle one.

1 2 3 4 5 6 7 8 9 10

Hypnotic Beatboxing formula or pattern I chose:_____________

How do you feel after doing the pattern or formula:____
____

Formula or pattern you want to try next:_______________________________

Notes:____
____
____
____
____
____
____

Fill In the Blank Worksheet

(Anxiety or Depression)

Date:_______Time:__________

Anxiety level 1 through 10. One is the least amount of anxiety 10 is the most circle one.

1 2 3 4 5 6 7 8 9 10

Hypnotic Beatboxing formula or pattern I chose:_____________

How do you feel after doing the pattern or formula:____

____

Formula or pattern you want to try next:___________________________

Notes:_______________________________________

____

____

____

____

____

____

Fill In the Blank Worksheet

(Anxiety or Depression)

Date:_______Time:__________

Anxiety level 1 through 10. One is the least amount of anxiety 10 is the most circle one.

1 2 3 4 5 6 7 8 9 10

Hypnotic Beatboxing formula or pattern I chose:_____________

How do you feel after doing the pattern or formula:____

____

Formula or pattern you want to try next:______________________________

Notes:___________________________________

____

____

____

____

____

____

Fill In the Blank Worksheet

(Anxiety or Depression)

Date:______Time:________

Anxiety level 1 through 10. One is the least amount of anxiety 10 is the most circle one.

1 2 3 4 5 6 7 8 9 10

Hypnotic Beatboxing formula or pattern I chose:____________

How do you feel after doing the pattern or formula:_____________________________________

____

Formula or pattern you want to try next:________________________

Notes:_______________________________________

____

____

____

____

____

____

Fill In the Blank Worksheet

(Anxiety or Depression)

Date:_______Time:__________

Anxiety level 1 through 10. One is the least amount of anxiety 10 is the most circle one.

1 2 3 4 5 6 7 8 9 10

Hypnotic Beatboxing formula or pattern I chose:______________

How do you feel after doing the pattern or formula:____

____

Formula or pattern you want to try next:____________________________

Notes:____

____

____

____

____

____

____

Fill In the Blank Worksheet

(Anxiety or Depression)

Date:_______Time:__________

Anxiety level 1 through 10. One is the least amount of anxiety 10 is the most circle one.

1 2 3 4 5 6 7 8 9 10

Hypnotic Beatboxing formula or pattern I chose:_____________

How do you feel after doing the pattern or formula:____

____

Formula or pattern you want to try next:_______________________________

Notes:____

____
____
____
____
____
____

Fill In the Blank Worksheet

(Anxiety or Depression)

Date:________Time:__________

Anxiety level 1 through 10. One is the least amount of anxiety 10 is the most circle one.

1 2 3 4 5 6 7 8 9 10

Hypnotic Beatboxing formula or pattern I chose:_____________

How do you feel after doing the pattern or formula:____

____

Formula or pattern you want to try next:_______________________

Notes:_____________________________________

____

____

____

____

____

____

Fill In the Blank Worksheet

(Anxiety or Depression)

Date:________Time:__________

Anxiety level 1 through 10. One is the least amount of anxiety 10 is the most circle one.

1 2 3 4 5 6 7 8 9 10

Hypnotic Beatboxing formula or pattern I chose:_____________

How do you feel after doing the pattern or formula:____

____

Formula or pattern you want to try next:_______________________________

Notes:____

____
____
____
____
____
____

Fill In the Blank Worksheet

(Anxiety or Depression)

Date:_______Time:__________

Anxiety level 1 through 10. One is the least amount of anxiety 10 is the most circle one.

1 2 3 4 5 6 7 8 9 10

Hypnotic Beatboxing formula or pattern I chose:_____________

How do you feel after doing the pattern or formula:____
____

Formula or pattern you want to try next:______________________________

Notes:____
____
____
____
____
____
____

Fill In the Blank Worksheet

(Anxiety or Depression)

Date:________Time:__________

Anxiety level 1 through 10. One is the least amount of anxiety 10 is the most circle one.

1 2 3 4 5 6 7 8 9 10

Hypnotic Beatboxing formula or pattern I chose:_______________

How do you feel after doing the pattern or formula:____

____

Formula or pattern you want to try next:_________________________

Notes:_______________________________________

____
____
____
____
____
____

Fill In the Blank Worksheet

(Anxiety or Depression)

Date:_______Time:_________

Anxiety level 1 through 10. One is the least amount of anxiety 10 is the most circle one.

1 2 3 4 5 6 7 8 9 10

Hypnotic Beatboxing formula or pattern I chose:_____________

How do you feel after doing the pattern or formula:____

____

Formula or pattern you want to try next:______________________________

Notes:____

____

____

____

____

____

____

Fill In the Blank Worksheet

(Anxiety or Depression)

Date:________Time:___________

Anxiety level 1 through 10. One is the least amount of anxiety 10 is the most circle one.

1 2 3 4 5 6 7 8 9 10

Hypnotic Beatboxing formula or pattern I chose:______________

How do you feel after doing the pattern or formula:____

____

Formula or pattern you want to try next:______________________________

Notes:____

____
____
____
____
____
____

Fill In the Blank Worksheet

(Anxiety or Depression)

Date:________Time:___________

Anxiety level 1 through 10. One is the least amount of anxiety 10 is the most circle one.

1 2 3 4 5 6 7 8 9 10

Hypnotic Beatboxing formula or pattern I chose:_____________

How do you feel after doing the pattern or formula:____
____

Formula or pattern you want to try next:______________________________

Notes:____

____

____

____

____

____

____

Notes:____

Notes:

Notes:____

Other Work by Michael Bolton Jr.

Writings

- **Two Sounds at Once – Michael Bolton Jr.**
- **Bioboxics -A Beginner's Guide -Michael Bolton Jr.**

Audio

"Tripped Out Pond" The Music Album

"Common Songbirds by Voice" Tutorials

"Minnesota Frog and Toad Calls by Voice" Tutorials

"The Bioboxics Breathing Technique" Tutorials

"The Pneumoboxics Technique" Tutorials

For Videos "Two Sounds at Once" YouTube

References

Helping Yourself with Autogenics

Two Sounds at Once-YouTube

Two Sounds at Once-Facebook

www.humanbeatbox.com

Michael Bolton Jr. is a Beatboxer and Author. His works include, "Two Sounds at Once", and "Bioboxics a Beginner's Guide". His most recent album is "Tripped Out Pond" He has presented on Hypnotic Beatboxing and related projects and has won talent shows for his skills as a beatboxer. He and his family live in Minnesota.